The Major League Way to Play Baseball

The Major League Way to Play
BASEBALL

by Bob Carroll

Simon & Schuster Books for Young Readers
Published by Simon & Schuster
NEW YORK / LONDON / TORONTO / SYDNEY / TOKYO / SINGAPORE

To the major leaguers of the 21st century,

in hopes that this book helped them get there.

A BASEBALL INK BOOK

Photo credits appear on page 88.

SIMON & SCHUSTER
BOOKS FOR YOUNG READERS
Simon & Schuster Building
Rockefeller Center
1230 Avenue of the Americas
New York, NY 10020

Also available in a LITTLE SIMON paperback edition.

Manufactured in the United States of America
1 3 5 7 9 10 8 6 4 2

Library of Congress Cataloging-in-Publication Data

Carroll, Bob. The major league way to play baseball.
(An Official major league baseball® book)
Summary: An introduction to baseball covering all the key aspects
of the game in question and answer format. 1. Baseball—Miscellanea—Juvenile literature.
[1. Baseball. 2. Questions and answers.] I. Title. II. Series.
GV867.5.C37 199 796.357 — dc20 90-41856
ISBN 0-671-73316-8
ISBN 0-671-70441-9 (pbk)

CONTENTS

ACKNOWLEDGMENTS

I would like to thank a great number of people for helping get this book out of the on-deck circle and up to bat. First of all, the many major leaguers who gave their tips—I won't name them all here because their names come up later—but I want to say one thing: the old saw about "the bigger they are, the nicer they are" certainly proved true. Others who were particularly helpful included David Falkner, author of *Nine Sides of the Diamond*, Brian Bartoe, Manager of Public Relations for the St. Louis Cardinals; Rick Cerrone, Vice President Public Relations for the Pittsburgh Pirates; David Alworth, Director of Publishing for Major League Baseball; and Chuck Cottier, coach for the Chicago Cubs (and a heck of an infielder in his day).

Several other public relations people deserve mentioning: Dick Bresciani (Boston Red Sox), Rick Vaughn (Baltimore Orioles), Matt Fisher (San Francisco Giants), Jay Alves (Oakland Athletics), Mike Williams (Los Angeles Dodgers), Dean Vogelaar (Kansas City Royals), Tom Mee (Minnesota Twins), and Jay Horwitz (New York Mets).

Thanks also to our player models: Kathleen Bernard, Michael Hall, Charles Monroe, Cory Smith, and Isaac Thorn.

Last, but certainly not least, John Thorn and Richard Puff of Baseball Ink and Sue Carroll of KDKA-TV for their irreplaceable support.

Bob Carroll

Introduction

The purpose of this book is to help you play better baseball. What you'll find in these pages is a great deal of advice and a great number of tips on how to improve your game. The advisers and tippers are major league players, past and present—the people who do it best. I've tried to ask the questions you'd ask them if you were standing in front of them. Sometimes I've given you the exact words of individual players; sometimes I've taken what several different players had to say and combined their ideas into a single explanation. But always I've looked for the best way to tell you how to do it.

Although I've talked to many different players about hitting, baserunning, playing all the positions in the field, and even strategy, there are three messages that all major league players have for you:

- Practice, practice, practice!
- There's no such thing as a "natural" except in the movies.
- Every player who ever got to the big leagues earned his way by hard work.

Practice and play safely! As important as baseball is, it's not worth risking your health over. If you follow a few simple safety rules, you'll be all right.

PART 1

The Offense

Ted Williams was constantly asked his advice on hitting, so he wrote a book about it, The Science of Hitting.

CHAPTER 1

Hitting

After Babe Ruth hit 60 home runs in 1927, he was asked how he did it. "I pick out a good one and I sock it," he said.

Accurate, no doubt, but not much help to a young hitter.

Neither was the famous explanation of turn-of-the-century phenomenon, Wee Willie Keeler, who hit as high as .424: "I hit 'em where they ain't."

Only slightly more useful were the comments of two nineteenth century stars: Jesse Burkett, who twice hit over .400, and Dan Brouthers, who had a lifetime batting average of .342. Burkett said hitting required "the old con-fee-dence," and Brouthers advised batters to "keep yer eye on the ball."

Modern players discuss hitting in far more detail. Ted Williams, baseball's last .400 hitter (.406 in 1941), was always willing to talk hitting with young players. And they constantly sought his advice. He wrote a whole book about his way: *The Science of Hitting*. Many of today's best hitters can cite Williams, chapter and verse.

Another book about hitting was authored by Hank Aaron after the 1973 season, when he stood poised at 713 career home runs—one short of Babe Ruth's lifetime total. "Hammerin' Hank" continued *Hitting the Aaron Way* for several more years to finish with the all-time major league career high of 755 homers.

Curiously the most influential batting guru for today's players was only a .255 lifetime hitter and spent most of his career on the bench. But if Charlie Lau was not a great hitter himself, he was a great teacher of hitting. He studied the art (or science) of hitting as no one else ever had and imparted his accumulated wisdom to such superstars as George Brett, whose .390 batting average in 1980 is the closest any major leaguer since Ted Williams has come to hitting .400.

Lau died in 1984, but his hitting theories live on with countless batting coaches in the major and minor leagues. Walt Hriniak, batting coach for the Chicago White Sox, is perhaps his most outspoken disciple.

Some kids are good hitters from the first time they pick up a bat. Others need some help. But everyone can benefit from a few good tips.

name is stamped on it. He may be terrific with that bat, but he's built differently from you. You need a bat that you can handle.

Don't make the mistake of thinking the heaviest bat in the rack will produce the longest hits. If you can't swing it easily, that heavy bat will only produce strikeouts.

Experiment. Take your stance with different bats. Start with a fairly heavy one. When you swing hard, does it pull you off balance? Is it too heavy? Now work your way down. Once you find a bat you can swing at top speed, you have the right weight. There's no reason to go lighter.

If you like to stand up close to the plate, you'll get a lot of pitches on the inside. A thicker handle can give you a little more wood (or aluminum) on the ball.

The length of the bat will affect how fast and how well you can swing it. The shorter the bat, the easier it is to control. But there's something else to remember here. You have to be able to cover the whole plate with your swing. That depends on both the length of the bat and how close you stand to the plate. If you're in your normal stance and still can't reach a knee-high strike on the outside corner, your bat's too short.

Keep the Label Up

Manufacturers stamp their names on the "top" of the bat to help batters. When the label is "up," the best wood is in "front"—the "sweet spot" on the bat. You'll get longer hits (and break fewer bats) with the label "up." You can test it by taking your normal stance and swinging to the point where the bat is over the plate. The label should be staring right back at you.

Unless you're Ted Williams: "I often swung with the label down so I couldn't see it." He did this, he said, because he didn't want *any* distractions. Of course, putting the label down instead of up still keeps the "good wood" in front.

Waiting on Deck

Get loose, get strong, and get an idea.

Get loose: You can get pretty stiff sitting on the bench waiting for your turn at bat. Kneel in the on-

Bats come in a wide variety of sizes and weights. Be sure to select one that's comfortable.

It's a good idea to stretch and get loose while waiting on deck.

deck circle and loosen up with a few stretching exercises.

Get strong: You can actually fool your body into thinking your bat is even lighter than it is. If your team has a "doughnut"—a heavy metal cylinder that slides onto the bat—take some practice swings with it on your bat. Some teams have an extra-heavy bat with lead in the barrel. If all else fails, try swinging two or three bats gathered in a bundle. When you go to bat after swinging all that extra weight around, your regular bat will feel light as a feather.

Get an idea: Perhaps the most important thing for you to do on the bench and in the on-deck circle is watch the opposing pitcher and think. How fast is he throwing? Does he change speeds a lot? Does his ball *do* anything? Don't wait until you're in the batter's box to start your at bat. Remember, the pitcher is going to try to fool you. That's his job. But if you know what kind of pitches he can throw *before* you go to bat, he's going to have a hard time taking you by surprise.

The Stance

When you take that bat in your hands, remember two things: First, you don't want to squeeze the life out of it; second, it isn't made of glass. In other words, don't grip it too tightly or too loosely. If you squeeze too hard, your swing will be tight and awkward; if you squeeze too little, you'll lose control of the bat. As in so many things, the middle road is best—a comfortable, firm grip.

Don't hold the bat pressed clear back in the crotch of the hand between the thumb and first finger. If you do, you'll actually put a little wave in your swing because your wrists will lock. When you hold a bat correctly, the second knuckles of your fingers should be lined up from the little finger of your bottom hand right up to the first finger of your top hand.

Should I choke up on the bat? Maybe. It depends on you. The bat has to feel comfortable in your hands. By choking—moving your grip up the

Some players prefer to choke up on the bat handle to gain better bat control.

Other players prefer to keep their hands down on the bat knob.

handle—you redistribute the weight of the bat and change the feel of it. The biggest advantage hitters who choke up find is that they can get around faster on a pitch. If you're consistently swinging late on good fastballs, definitely try choking up.

But there are two disadvantages. First, by choking up, you "shorten" the bat. You may not be able to reach pitches on the outside corner without moving a little closer to the plate. Second, you probably won't be able to drive the ball quite as far if you choke up. Almost all home run hitters hold the bat down on the end. Choke-hitters are usually going for singles. They give up a little power for better bat control.

The key here is to know yourself. If you're strong enough to control the bat and get around on fast pitches while holding the bat down at the end, there's no reason to choke up. But if you swing a little late or need more control of the bat, choking up is worth trying. Many hitters hold the bat down at the end until they have two strikes, then choke up a little.

Where should I stand in the batter's box?

Williams advises batters to stand deep: "I see no advantage whatsoever in being way up front, with your lead foot ahead of the plate, because you are shortening the distance to the pitcher and cheating yourself."

Obviously the important question is whether you can reach every pitch in the strike zone with good wood. An easy way to measure this is to stand at the plate and extend the bat held in your "front" hand (the left hand if you're a righthanded batter) until you can touch the middle of the plate. If you have to stretch or bend way forward, you're too far from the plate. It's all right if you bend forward a little; just don't bend clear into something that's completely away from your natural batting stance.

You still may have to shift a little to get the distance just right. If all you can do with a pitch on the outside corner is foul it off, you're probably too far from the plate. If you hit pitches on the inside corner with only the handle of the bat, you're too close.

Is there one "best" batting stance? You're go-

The best way to determine if you're too far from the plate is to stand where you usually do and place your bat in the middle of the plate. If you have to stretch, you're too far away. If you're comfortable, you're probably just right.

Two of the different ways you can stand at the plate are the open stance (left) and the closed stance (right).

ing to be tempted to stand up there the way your favorite player does. But what's right for him may be all wrong for you. Major leaguers have had years and years to discover just what works best for their particular body types and strengths. And even then many players change their batting stances in the course of a career, a season, or even a game. Your favorite player is probably taller and heavier than you. Certainly at this stage, he's stronger.

Again, experimentation is a good idea. You should try many different stances as you look for the one that's perfect for you. But go about it scientifically. Don't start with some strange extreme and hope to find an answer. You may never get there. Start with a normal, "medium" stance. Then try variations one at a time: you might try a more open position, a slight crouch, a longer stride. If it doesn't work for you, then you can easily go back to your basic stance and start in a different direction.

What is a normal stance? A batter in a normal

stance keeps his weight balanced evenly on both feet. He's on the balls of his feet, not flat-footed. And his knees are slightly bent.

For starters place your feet about as wide apart as the width of your shoulders, although you may adjust this later.

Your feet should be parallel to the plate. In other words, if you draw a line from the tip of the toe of one shoe to the tip of the toe of your other shoe, it will run right alongside—never getting closer or farther away from—the line made by the side edge of the plate.

What are "open" and "closed" stances? The terms "open stance" and "closed stance" refer to the feet. Stand with your front foot farther from the plate than your back foot and you have an open stance. With your front foot closer to the plate, you "close" your stance.

Some batters prefer a closed stance because they feel they can get more power into their swing by

Your back elbow should be at about a forty-five degree angle from your body.

cocking their body away from the pitch. The disadvantage is that they sometimes can't see the ball as well. An open stance allows a batter to see the ball better (he's turned more toward the pitcher) but may reduce his power and also may pull him away from the plate. If you start with your feet parallel, you can experiment by opening or closing your stance, yet easily move back to the middle ground.

Whether your stance is open or closed, your stride should be toward the pitch.

Should I crouch or stand up straight? Charlie Lau was against standing up straight because he felt it made batters tense. There are good hitters who crouch way over with very bent knees and hips, but, again, the way to start is in the middle, bent slightly—and comfortably—at the knees and hips.

Should one of my shoulders be higher than the other? No, keep your shoulders parallel to the ground. If you raise your back shoulder, you'll either twist your body away from the pitcher, making it harder to follow the pitch, or you'll be forced to have your weight shifted onto your front foot.

Either way your swing will probably be a big loop and you'll have trouble ever meeting a good pitch.

If you raise your front shoulder, you'll lose power and almost certainly uppercut your swing.

Where should my back elbow be? Batting coaches used to teach hitters to hold their back elbow up in the air away from the body. They said it was to keep a hitter from having a "hitch" in his swing. But they were wrong. That extended elbow actually puts a hitch *into* a swing. A batter has to bring his elbow down to start his swing. This is wasted movement that slows the swing and distracts the hitter. The proper approach is to keep your back elbow down from the start. Then you can go straight into your swing.

The famous second baseman Joe Morgan used to take his stance and "flap" his back elbow up and down a couple of times before each pitch. He did it to remind himself to keep his elbow down. Did it work? Well, enough hits "flew" off his bat that he was twice voted the Most Valuable Player in his league, and he wound up in the Hall of Fame.

How should I hold my hands? We already mentioned gripping the bat so that the second knuckles on your hands line up. When you take your stance, keep your hands back (about even with the armpit of your rear shoulder) and comfortably away from your body.

Should I hold the bat still? Lau suggested establishing rhythmic movements within your stance as the pitcher gets ready. Some players swing the bat a little, some wiggle it, some only wiggle their fingers. It's a timing device. But, as the pitch is delivered, keep that bat still.

At what angle should I hold the bat? Williams held his bat straight up and down because it felt lighter that way. Steve Garvey, an All Star first baseman with the Dodgers and Padres, held his bat the same way. But Lau thought up-and-down bats caused too many players to have hitches in their swings, making them slow in getting the bat around. He taught batters to hold the bat parallel to the ground, or at no more than about a forty-five-degree angle.

Jay Bell of the Pittsburgh Pirates offers an extreme example, "From the time I was in Little League, I always wanted to be like Steve Garvey and had my bat straight up and down. I was able to get away with it until I got to the major league level. But I couldn't get away with it there because I had a hitch in my swing. I wasn't catching up to the faster fastballs. So Pirate batting coach Milt May and I decided we'd get back to basics. I dropped the bat *on* my shoulder. It got rid of the hitch and enabled me to get around quicker."

Up at the Plate: The Strike Zone

To be a good hitter you must know the strike zone. You probably already have heard that the strike

The strike zone is the area above the plate from your armpits to your knees.

zone is the area over the plate, between your armpits and knees (when you are in your normal batting stance). But to *know* the strike zone means standing at the plate and judging whether a speeding pitch is going to pass through that area. That takes practice.

The whole reason for the strike zone is to define the area where a good batter should be able to hit a pitch. If you choose to swing at a pitch *out* of the strike zone, you're doing the pitcher a big favor. He *wants* you to swing at a bad pitch.

Obviously, any hitter—no matter how talented he is—can hit a pitch that's over the plate more often and with more authority than he can hit a pitch he has to strain to reach.

Aren't some batters "bad ball" hitters? Hall of Fame catcher Yogi Berra was a good hitter who often went after bad pitches. One time he swung and missed at a pitch over his head. As he came back to the dugout, he complained: "How can that pitcher stay in the league? His control is so bad!"

Batters have occasionally gotten hits on pitches out of the strike zone. But most of the time they made outs. Williams says: "The greatest hitter living can't hit bad balls good." Without a doubt, the "bad ball" hitters would have been even better hitters if they'd been strict "good ball" hitters. In fact, for all their famous "bad ball" hits, by far *most* of their hits came off good pitches in the strike zone.

How can I keep from swinging at bad pitches in practice? Even though it's practice, get a friend—one who understands the strike zone—to call balls and strikes. And that includes pitches you actually hit. Suppose you hit a little looper that falls just over the infield, but the pitch would have been a ball. Count your "hit" as an "out." Most of the time, when you swing at a "ball," an out is what you'll get.

You have to stand up at the plate and watch pitch after pitch. Sometimes a pitch will be so obviously out of the strike zone that you won't even move. Most times you'll see the pitch coming close enough that you'll start into your swing. Suddenly a little voice in your head shouts, "*No!*" and you stop. But, if the voice shouts, "*Yes!*" give it your best swing.

What if the umpire calls it wrong? Unfortunately no matter how good your "eye," once in a while a pitch that you are certain is a ball will be called a strike by the umpire. As a famous umpire once said, "It's nothing until I call it." Once the umpire's made his decision, he's not going to change it. That pitch is gone forever. So don't fret about it. The pitcher just loves to see you upset. While you're huffing and puffing, he's going to try to sneak *another* strike by you. So wake up. Concentrate on the pitch that's coming.

It won't hurt, though, to remember just where that last pitch was. The same umpire will probably call the next pitch in the same location a strike. And the pitcher, remembering that he "fooled" you there before, will probably try to throw another pitch right in that spot again. Look for it.

Up at the Plate: The Swing

The whole action of swinging at a pitch takes only a split second, but so much happens in that time that it will take several pages to explain it.

Divide the swing into five parts—stride, pivot, arms, wrists, and follow-through. The parts happen in series one after another, but they happen so fast and blend into one another so that there's no real distinction between them. While the parts are discussed one at a time, you should really be concerned with a smooth, fluid movement.

What is the stride? You should be standing with your feet apart about the width of your shoulders and your weight evenly distributed. You should be on the balls of your feet, not back on your heels. *As the pitcher delivers*, step forward toward the pitch with your front foot. Sounds simple, doesn't it?

Actually it's one of the hardest parts to learn.

How far should I stride? It depends on your height, build, and strength, but a couple of things are always true.

Try this. Take your normal stance and stride and then freeze. Have a friend walk up and give you a little push in the chest. If you start to topple over, your stride is too long. You're off balance. On the other hand, if you're solid as a rock, it's probably too

short. You need a stride somewhere in between those two extremes.

Incidentally, Charlie Lau recommended that the stride foot be turned in—slightly pigeon-toed—to help the batter see the ball better.

What should happen to my weight when I stride? Ted Williams advocated keeping your weight back until the last second, in other words, *after* the stride has been made. Dale Murphy of the Atlanta Braves agrees: "I'm a back-foot swinger." Williams hit over 500 home runs; Murphy has hit over 300.

On the other hand, Charlie Lau advocated starting the weight forward as soon as your stride foot touches the ground. Although there might be a slight loss in power, he felt there would be a far greater benefit in bat control and consistency.

Lau's method is the most popular in the majors today. Young hitters tend to do best when they let their weight shift *forward* to meet the ball. But *smoothly* forward! Don't lunge!

What is the pivot? Even as you're finishing your stride, your hips are coming around. It's called "opening up" your hips, but what it really is, is a sharp pivot with your middle body. Pivoting your hips so that your belt buckle is facing the pitcher is very important because much of your power comes from there. Furthermore, it turns you so that you can see the pitch better and also starts your arms in motion.

If your hips are locked or stiff, you can forget about hitting.

According to Williams, at the same time he strode forward, he cocked his hips backward—a slight turn with the middle of his body away. Then, as he started his swing, he'd pivot his hips forward, putting his whole body behind his swing.

You should try to make your pivot a smooth movement out of your stride, not a sudden, last-second jerk.

When do I move my arms? Your hip pivot starts your arms moving. You want a strong swing. Lau studied hundreds of films of outstanding batters. The one thing that they all had in common, he said,

Before you can have a good swing, you must be in position at the plate: knees bent slightly, weight evenly distributed, and relaxed.

When you start to swing, your bat at first goes backward and then comes forward with your weight being placed on your back foot.

In the middle of your swing your front arm is straight with your back arm slightly bent.

It's important that you follow through with your swing—don't stop your swing once you hit the ball.

Many of today's batting coaches follow the teachings of Charlie Lau.

One of the most important things to remember is always to wear a helmet when batting.

Safety First: Batting Helmets

Before you even grab a bat, grab a batting helmet. Safety is more important than anything else on a ballfield, but a good batting helmet can help you in another way. You'll feel a lot more confident standing in there against a good fastball if you know you're well protected. And, as Jesse Burkett said, confidence is one of the most important parts of hitting. You have to know you can do it.

When you choose your batting helmet, whether you're buying one for yourself or picking one from your team's stock, there are a couple of things you should look for. A safe batting helmet should be made with a good polycarbonate alloy shell, not just flimsy plastic. Inside there should be a double foam pad. One side absorbs any impact from the ball; the other makes the helmet fit snugly on your head. Snug, not tight. The helmet shouldn't wiggle or wobble when you swing the bat or run the bases, but if it's too tight it will distract you. (And worse, it won't do the job of protecting you from the impact of beanballs because a loose helmet won't absorb the force of a thrown baseball.)

Make sure it sits properly on your head. The earholes should be centered right over your ears, and there should be about two finger-widths of space between the bridge of your nose and the bill of the helmet.

Two other tips: Never wear a helmet that's cracked, and be very careful about painting your helmet. Some paints can actually soften the helmet and others can make it brittle.

An easy way to make sure you have a good, safe helmet is to look for the letters "NOCSAE" molded into the outside of the shell. That's not a brand name. NOCSAE is a company that tests sports equipment to see that it's up to snuff.

Choosing a Bat

The bat you choose can make a big difference in how well you hit. Some players think aluminum bats will drive a ball farther. Others say it doesn't matter, as long as you have the "right" bat for you. Good hitters from the earliest days have had favorite bats—bats they felt comfortable swinging. Never choose a bat just because your favorite player's was that when the front foot completed the stride, the hands and bat were still *back*. He called this the "launching position."

When you swing, extend your arms. That produces power. But never "swing from the heels" so that you're out of control. You still have to hit the ball.

Should I try to swing "up" to get the ball in the air? Williams favored a slightly upward angle. Hank Aaron said to hit down on the ball. Lau usually preferred a level swing.

But the differences were very slight—only a few degrees between Williams's "up" and Aaron's "down."

No good hitter ever suggested "uppercutting"— an extreme upward movement as if you were hitting uphill. Nor did they tell anyone to chop at the ball as if they were trying to drive it into the plate. Either way makes it unlikely you'll hit the ball at all because the bat is moving up toward the flight of the ball at an extreme angle. So there's only the tiniest fraction of a second when the ball and bat could meet.

A good, level swing works best for most batters. If you go into it with your second knuckles lined up and keep your shoulders level, a smooth, level swing should be the result.

How important is "wrist action"? As your bat comes around, you snap your wrists. That last little speeding up of the bat puts an amazing amount of power into your swing. You've seen players who seem to take an easy, almost effortless swing, yet drive the ball great distances. That comes from a strong wrist snap.

How can I test my "wrist action"? Here's an easy way. Go into your swing in slow motion. As you stride and pivot, your arms begin bringing the bat around. Now freeze! Your hands are in front of you, but your bat is still trailing behind, with the barrel pointing in the general direction of the catcher.

Now (if you're batting righthanded) your left hand stays in the same place while your right hand brings the bat the rest of the way to where it will meet the ball. As your right hand comes forward, you have to roll it over the left, but your swing will stay level if your second knuckles are properly lined up.

Where should my bat be when it meets the ball? You should find that the place where your right hand stops pushing the bat and begins to roll is just out in front of the plate. That's the spot where you want to meet the ball because that is where you have concentrated the most power. If you hit the ball while your bat is still "behind" the plate, your swing is still "getting up steam." If you're too far out in front, you'll either pop the ball off the end of your bat or miss it completely.

I keep hitting to the opposite field. What can I do? If you're always hitting to the opposite field, you're probably swinging a little late and meeting the ball behind the plate. You're not getting all your power into your hits. When you're hitting out in front properly, you'll pull most pitches slightly. *But don't force it.* Once you've mastered proper hitting techniques, you'll pull naturally.

I'm having trouble seeing the pitch. Can you help? Follow the pitch all the way from the pitcher's hand (even before he throws it) until you meet it with the sweet spot on your bat.

Dan Brouthers said, "Keep yer eye on the ball." That's only half the story. The whole truth is "keep your eyes on the ball." Both of them. Think we're joking? Try this test.

Close one eye. Then ask a friend standing in front of you to hold up one finger somewhere within your reach. Now swing your right arm out and try to bring your right index finger straight over to touch the tip of his finger. About half the time you'll miss by an inch or two. That's because you can't get much *depth perception* with only one eye. And if you can't always touch your friend's finger when it is stationary, what chance would you have swinging a bat at a moving baseball?

Amazingly enough, many young batters try to "hit with one eye." They have their head in such a position that they can see the ball with the eye nearest the pitcher. Their other eye is blocked by their nose.

A simple way to keep this from happening when you're in your stance is to put your chin on your leading shoulder. When you can feel the tip of your chin touching your shoulder, you'll find that your head is turned toward the pitcher so that you can see the ball coming with both eyes.

How can I keep from ducking my head away when I swing? Use your shoulder again. A common problem young players have is pulling their heads away as the ball approaches the plate. They see the first part of the ball's flight okay, but lose it at the last second. It's tempting to look where you want the ball to go, but if you do—it won't. You can break yourself of this bad habit by remembering that when you are into your follow-through, your chin should be touching your *other*, or trailing, shoulder.

If you use the shoulder-to-shoulder method (and don't close your eyes), you'll see the ball all the way, and your hitting will improve.

What good is a follow-through after I've already hit the ball? All right, after the ball flies off the bat, nothing you do from then on will make it go farther. However, the bat will continue around naturally *unless* you purposely stop it. And to stop it immediately after you hit the ball, you have to *start* stopping it *before* you hit the ball. So while a follow-through adds nothing to your batting, the *absence* of a follow-through can ruin it. Let your follow-through slow the bat naturally. Pivot on the heel of your front foot and the ball of your back foot. And end with your chin on your back shoulder.

Should I keep both hands on the bat when following through? Lau said no. He felt that keeping the top hand on the bat after contact, kept batters from extending their arms. He told batters to let loose with their top hand.

But hold on tight with your other hand! A flying bat is dangerous!

What's the most important thing—stride, pivot, arms, wrists, or follow-through? They're all important. But the *most* important thing is to watch the ball and only swing at strikes.

CHAPTER 2

Batting Practice and Other Drills

What batting drills can help me improve? The only complete and perfect batting drill is to actually stand at the plate and bat against real pitching. However, if that's not done right, it can do more harm than good.

First of all, you won't improve your hitting by standing there while pitch after pitch bounces in front of the plate or misses the strike zone by a mile. In fact, you may become so impatient that you'll start swinging at bad pitches, and that's a really bad habit. Usually, the best person to pitch batting practice is your coach or some older person who can get the ball over the plate.

Incidentally there's nothing wrong with standing up there to give one of your teammates practice at pitching to a batter, just don't think of it as *batting* practice, and don't swing at bad pitches.

Should I face fast pitching in practice? Since it's practice, you won't want your batting practice pitcher to throw you his best fastball, but you don't want him to throw you "baby pitches" either. Generally it's best to start with pitches about three-quarters as fast as you'll see in a game. Once you start timing them, your pitcher can begin throwing a little faster.

How long should I bat in practice? Don't monopolize the batting box. In the first place all your teammates will get bored standing around. But just as important, you won't improve by taking a long at bat because you'll usually just keep doing the same things, right or wrong. Take about ten swings and then get out of there so you can think about what you just did.

Once you've had time to think it through, you're ready to bat again. It's better to have many short practice at bats than one long one.

Besides actually batting are there any other useful drills? There are a few good batting drills. These include:

The Phantom At Bat. Some batters find it useful to stand behind a batting cage where they can see pitches and then swing or not, depending on whether the pitch is a strike. This may help you

Working with a batting tee is one of the most useful ways to correct problems in your swing and also to practice a level swing.

learn the strike zone if you're ruthlessly honest about whether a pitch you've just swung at was a strike.

Here's Looking At You, Kid. Dave Winfield suggests: "Use a mirror to study your stance, swing, and follow-through and see if you are swinging smoothly and cleanly. Be careful with the bat; don't break the mirror."

Done to a Tee. Hitting off a batting tee or against a toss thrown easily from the side (by an adult only!) can help a coach study your swing, although it won't help your timing. Better than a tee or toss for this drill is to have a coach stand off to the side with a piece of garden hose that's been taped about two-thirds of its length, making that part of it stiff. The coach holds the stiff part and dangles the loose end in the strike zone while the batter swings at the end. Put a piece of tape around the loose end so you'll have a specific target to swing at.

You can do this exercise in a confined space because there's no ball flying out. It also allows the coach to put the "ball" exactly where he wants it, so you can practice hitting high, low, inside, or outside "pitches."

Major League Hitting Tips

Choosing A Bat

"You don't have to go to the plate with a bat that's too big and heavy just to prove you can swing it," says former All Star first baseman Steve Garvey. "You'll have a smoother swing and get more hits with the right sized bat."

Dave Clark of the Chicago Cubs adds: "Try a lot of different sizes. Avoid a bat that's too long, too short, or too heavy. Light is right."

Mike Scioscia of the Los Angeles Dodgers has an interesting way of choosing a bat: "From the time I was a boy, I've been taught to select my bat by starting at the handle. You've got to get the feel of the bat in your hands. By that I mean you've got to choose how it feels when you grip it. You've got to see whether you do better with a thick handle or a thin one.

"Worry about the weight of the bat later. Look at the handle. Get the feel. Then you decide on the barrel and what thickness you want there."

The Stance

"Every batter has a different stance," Dave Winfield of the California Angels cautions. "Find one that is comfortable for you. Don't copy someone else's stance."

Ted Williams: "Your weight should be balanced, distributed evenly on both feet, and slightly forward on the balls of the feet, with the knees bent and flexible."

But, Dave Winfield says, "Don't wiggle the bat as the pitch is thrown. Keep the bat still. Many players shake the bat as the pitcher winds up, but the bat should be still as he releases the ball. Keep your head still. Moving the head takes your eyes off the ball. Concentrate on the ball before you start moving the bat."

Know the Strike Zone

Williams: "A good hitter can hit a pitch that is over the plate three times better than a great hitter (can hit) a questionable ball in a tough spot."

Steve Garvey confides: "I didn't get a single hit my first year in Little League, but I walked a lot."

Hitting

"Don't overstride," Dave Winfield says. "A batter should always be in position to adjust to the pitch. Move your front leg slightly as the ball approaches. Use your stride to move to the pitch. For example: if the pitch is coming over the outside of the plate, move your front foot in.

"A good batter always tries to get the most out of each swing. Extend your arms. This gives you more power with the bat. Swing smoothly through the ball."

Ty Cobb (top) and Lou Brock (bottom) were two of the game's greatest basestealers. Cobb's 892 stolen bases was for years the American League record until Rickey Henderson passed him in 1990. Brock holds the National League record with 938 stolen bases.

CHAPTER 3

Baserunning

Everybody wants to get on base, but a lot of young players aren't always sure what to do once they get there. Smart baserunning is often the difference between winning and losing a game. Mistakes on the basepaths can be embarrassing and can hurt your team. Some mistakes can be dangerous.

Of course, before you can run the bases, you have to *get* on base. When you hit the ball, don't stand there and admire its flight. Get down to first base as fast as you can.

Can I improve my speed? No. But you might not be running at your best speed right now. For instance, when you run, do your heels hit the ground? When you push off the toes of your left foot and stretch your right leg, does the heel of your right foot hit the ground first, then the sole of your right foot? As you move forward, do you roll up onto the toes of your right foot and push off again? All that takes time. Heel-to-toe running isn't running at all; it's fast walking. You should learn to run on your toes—or to be exact, on the balls and toes of your feet—like a sprinter. This will actually shorten your stride, but your feet will move much faster—and so will you.

Running in this way will force you to lean forward, and that will increase your speed too. No one runs fast standing straight up.

But keep your head up. You have to be able to see the play developing in front of you.

Another little tip is to pump your arms forward and back, not across your chest. Where the head and hands go, the feet will follow.

Once you're running correctly, practice, practice, practice until it becomes second nature to you.

Isn't it a waste to run hard to first on an obvious out? Wrong! There is absolutely no excuse ever to loaf to first on any batted ball. If it's mishandled, you'll be safe and may be able to get to second. If it's caught and your running was wasted, so what? You've lost nothing and had some good exercise.

And pay attention to where you run. Halfway down the first base line, about eighteen inches in foul territory, another invisible line leads down to

When running to first base you must stay in the running lane.

first base. The runner is supposed to run inside the space between this line and the foul line.

Why must a runner stay to the outside of the baseline? There are three good reasons for forcing the runner to keep to the outside of the baseline on his way to first base. First, if the ball is hit just in front of the plate, the catcher must be allowed to throw it to the first baseman without the runner unfairly blocking his throw. Second, it's safer for the runner who might otherwise get hit in the back with a baseball. And third, by running to first on the outside of the line, the runner will naturally step on the outside of the base as he crosses it. This is important because on any close play the fielder will also have his foot on the bag at the same time. When the fielder touches the inside of the base and the runner steps on the outside, everything is fine. But if they both go for the middle of the bag, someone could trip or get stepped on.

When the play is close, should I jump for the base at the end? Run straight through the bag on any play you think will be close. No matter how "bang-bang" you think the play is going to be, don't *leap* for first. Breaking your stride like that actually slows you down by a split second. It also makes it harder for you to turn toward second on an overthrow. Finally, leaps like that sometimes lead to pulled muscles.

Which way should I turn after crossing the base? Always run aggressively. But on a close play at first, unless you hear your coach yelling for you to go for second—probably because of an overthrow—turn to your *right* after you cross the bag. If you turn *left*, the umpire may think you're trying for second, and you can be put out.

And keep your eye on the ball!

If you hit the ball to the outfield, be sure to find it with your eyes as soon as you can. Even a routine "flare" may be booted, allowing you an extra base.

"Belly out" before you get to first. This means that as you near the bag—about fifteen feet away—move slightly to your right so you can cut the corner and head for second if you get the chance. "Bellying out" is something you should do when approaching second or third, too.

Are there any rules about leading off base? Before you get to first, you should already know the rules you're playing under. Ask your coach. Some youth leagues allow runners to lead off bases at any time. Others permit leading off only after the pitch is past the batter. Under these rules a runner leading off early won't be called out for it, but he can end up being sent back to his base on a play where he would otherwise have advanced.

What should I look for before leading off? Be aware of where the ball is. Never lead off until you actually see that the pitcher is holding it and standing on the pitching rubber. Stand there with your left foot on the base. What could be more embarrassing than walking off base only to find the fielder has pulled the old "hidden ball" trick to put you out? Once you know the ball is far away, look at your coach for a second. Then, as you start to lead off, listen to your coach, but watch the ball.

How far should I lead off? You learn what's the proper lead for you through practice and repetition. Some players have quick feet; others have slow feet. Through practice you learn what you can do. A good average lead off first base for a beginner is four steps—two steps and a slide back.

What's my "leading off stance"? When leading off you face the pitcher. Your feet are spread comfortably apart, knees bent, hands out and low. Your weight is usually evenly distributed.

As you set up in your lead, you move laterally like a crab, with short steps, not crossing one leg over the other. This is something you should practice. Naturally, once you're committed to running, you push off on the foot nearest the base, cross over with your other leg, and put it in high gear.

The pitcher tries to pick me off. Should I slide back headfirst? An attempted pickoff is the *only* time it's okay for a runner your age to use a headfirst slide. Sometimes that's the only way to get back to

When leading off first, you should remain close enough to the base to get back safely.

Returning to first base on a pickoff throw is the only time you should dive headfirst into a base.

the base fast enough, but it's still the "slide of last resort." Sliding back to the base headfirst puts your head very near where the throw is coming and puts your fingers right where they may get stepped on. If you know you can get back with a feetfirst slide (or no slide at all), avoid a headfirst slide.

Should I lead off second as far as I lead off first? You can get a slightly longer lead off second base than off first because the shortstop and second baseman play farther away from second base than the first baseman plays from first. But so what? Unless you're planning on stealing third, there's not much advantage to a long lead at second. With a normal lead you'll usually be able to score on any safe hit to the outfield. And you can get back to second to tag up easily on a long fly. Be alert. Even

When you run the bases, always remember to lean over slightly and pump with your arms. You also should be looking straight ahead.

though the fielders are normally farther from the base than you are, you can't afford to fall asleep out there or they'll sneak in behind you for a pickoff.

Is there anything different about my lead off third? When you reach third base, be sure to take your lead in foul territory. If you stand in fair territory and a batted ball hits you, you're out.

Don't turn your back on the catcher when returning to the base. He can whip the ball down to the third baseman and you can be tagged out.

What are the "basics" about when to run and when not to? Be sure you know how many outs there are. With two outs run every time the ball is hit. Listen to your coach; he'll help you.

As the pitch is thrown, you must watch to see where it's hit. On popups to the infielders, the rule is simple: with none out or one out, *don't run.* No matter how many outs there are, if the ball is hit on the ground when you're on first, you have no choice. *Run*!

And if the ball is hit to the outfield safely, you also must run.

What do I do when the ball is hit to the outfield? Problems start when the ball is hit to the outfield and you're not certain whether it will be caught or not. If you run to second and it's caught, you can be put out when the ball is thrown to first base before you can return. If you play it too safe and stay on first base, you might not be able to get to second on a safe hit if the outfielder fields it quickly. Your best bet is to go about halfway to second until you see what's going to happen. Don't go quite so far on a ball hit to right field as you go on a ball hit to left because the right fielder's throw is shorter to first.

If I'm on second, must I always run on groundballs? When you're at second base, you must be aware of the situation. With a runner behind you on first base, you're forced to run on any groundball.

But with no runner on first and fewer than two out, you have a choice on a grounder. Normally you won't have trouble reaching third on a groundball hit to second or first base because the fielders would have to make a very long throw across the diamond. But on any grounder hit in front of you to the shortstop or third baseman, be sure the ball has gone through to the outfield before you run.

If I'm on second, what do I do on flyballs? Generally you play flyballs the same when you're on second as when you're on first, with this exception: on a ball hit deep, go *back* to the base. If the ball falls in safely, you'll be able to score easily; if it's caught, you may be able to tag up and get to third.

Should I lead off third base? If you reach third base, it's a good idea to call time and talk the situation over with the coach. Consider all the possibilities.

Once you take your lead, listen to the coach. If a ball is hit on the ground to the left side of the diamond, he will be in a better position to see the play developing than you are. If he says run, *do it!*

Tag up on any flyball that can possibly be caught. If it falls in for a hit, you can walk home. (But don't walk. Run!)

Should I always try to score on a flyout? If a fly is caught, use some judgment before dashing for home. How fast are you? How deep is it? How well can the outfielder throw? How many outs are there? Who's the next batter? For example, if a short fly is the first out of the inning and a good hitter is coming up, it probably isn't worth the risk to try to tag up and run.

Remember, you're only forced to run if runners are on *both* first base and second base behind you.

Must I wait until I get a steal sign? You always must know if you're *allowed* to steal. Some managers prefer to have their runners steal only when given a sign. Others let the players decide on their own. If you're not certain what your manager wants, don't wait until you're on base to ask.

Are there "bad" times to try to steal? The first rule of stealing bases is don't try to steal if there is a runner on the base in front of you (unless, of course, your manager has ordered a double steal). This may sound so obvious as to be funny, but even a few professional players (very few!) have tried to steal an occupied base. They simply weren't paying attention to the situation.

The game situation can affect whether to steal or not. For example, if your team is several runs behind, it might not be a good time to take a chance, especially with no outs in the inning. On the other hand, a good baserunner can sometimes ignite a big inning.

I want to steal second. How can I tell when to go? Most successful base stealers concentrate on the pitcher's knees. If they watch his hands or eyes, they can be fooled and picked off, but the knees never lie. The rules state that when the pitcher moves the knee toward home plate, he must pitch the ball. And that's the runner's cue to head for second base.

Can I tell whether to slide by watching the fielder? If there's a fielder waiting at the base, slide. Oh, sure, it's always possible that the catcher saw you had the base and decided not to throw. The fielder may be faking. So what? You've got the base. A more likely fake is for the fielder to stand there as though no throw is coming. He wants you to run in standing up (and slowing down so you won't overrun the base). Then at the last second, he'll catch the throw and slap the ball on you. Don't chance it. If the bag is covered, slide.

Should I try to steal third? Third base is not stolen as often as second. Some players say it's an easier base to steal, even though the catcher has a shorter throw. They say they have an advantage because they can get a longer lead off second. The big question is, how much better off are you at third than at second? Second base still puts you in "scoring position" where you can make it home on most basehits.

The greatest advantage to being on third is the possibility of scoring on a flyball out. But remember, that only applies if there are fewer than two outs. An old baseball saying is "Never make the third out of an inning at third base." That means, among other things, don't try to steal third with two outs unless you absolutely *know* you can make it.

Is trying to steal home a good idea? Lee Lacy, who stole nearly 200 bases during sixteen seasons in the major leagues, says: "I'm not too keen about stealing home. It's too dangerous. When you do, you've got to get one heck of a jump on the pitcher. The third base coach can be a help. But I'm no advocate of stealing home."

Of course, many leagues for kids prohibit stealing home anyway.

When should I slide? Slides are spectacular. However, never slide unless there's a good reason. First of all you could be hurt. Secondly it puts you down on the ground for a few seconds when you might otherwise take advantage of a misplay by the defense to get an extra base.

But once you decide to slide, *don't change your mind.* A "half-slide" is the easiest way in the world to get hurt. Think about it. You're running full tilt and you start to go into a slide. You're off-balance and suddenly decide to stay up. You can twist a knee or an ankle, or you can fall right on your nose.

How can I avoid scrapes? Before sliding into a real base in a real game, you should have put in plenty of practice time learning to do it safely. Even then you can get some pretty good scrapes from sliding on a hard infield. Special sliding pads are made to prevent this, but if you don't have pads, an old pair of jeans worn under your uniform (or two pairs of trousers when you're not in uniform) will help a lot.

If you don't have a sliding pit—a place with sand or soft earth—to practice sliding in, find a nice grassy spot in the outfield.

Why should I slide? There are two advantages to slides if they're done properly. First they make it harder for the fielder to tag the runner. Second they keep the runner from "overrunning the base," that

is, going completely past the base and getting tagged out. With practice you will learn just how far from the base to start your slide.

What are the different kinds of slides? There are four basic slides—the popup, the hook, the hand tag, and the headfirst—three to practice and one to avoid.

First the one to avoid: the headfirst slide. We've already said that the only excuse for a headfirst slide is to get back to a base. Then it's more like "lying down" to the base. We still don't like it for young players. And neither will you if a fielder steps on your hand.

A headfirst slide when running to a base has the disadvantage of putting your head close to the throw and your fingers close to an opponent's feet. Additionally you can jam your wrist or shoulder when you hit the ground or the base. Will you get to the base faster than with a feetfirst slide? No. Can you get up and run quicker on an overthrow? No. Is it harder for a fielder to tag you? It's true that tagging a hand is slightly more difficult than tagging a foot (because a hand is smaller), but tagging a foot is more intimidating, so no. Are there *any* advantages to a headfirst slide? No.

What about the popup slide? The popup slide is made straight into the base and lets the runner "pop up" to run to the next base. Drop to the seat of your pants—a little more on one hip—and slide straight into the base. Your legs are stretched out but bent slightly. Don't keep your legs locked because you can be hurt if you slam into a base with your leg rigid. Keep your knees bent. Stay flat. Give the fielder a small target and slide under his tag. Keep your hands out of the way by holding your arms back over your head with your fingers in a fist. Some runners carry a handful of dirt to remind them to clench their fists to avoid catching a finger.

What's a hook slide? The hook slide can be made either to the left or the right. We'll describe a "right hook" as though you're running to second on a ball hit to the left side of the infield. The second baseman moves in front of the bag to take the throw, so

When you slide straight into the base, your momentum allows you to pop up once you hit the base.

Your inside foot hooks around the corner of the bag when you use a hook slide.

you want to hook into the right corner of the bag.

Drop to the seat of your pants with your right leg folded under your left. Your left foot goes past the bag on the outfield side. And you "hook" the bag with the toe of your right foot.

A variation on the hook is to slide a little farther to the right with your legs spread. This way you hook the bag with your left toe. This way is a little harder to do, but it presents the fielder with an even smaller target for a tag.

How about the hand-tag slide? The hand-tag is not much different from the hook slide. In this one you slide a little farther out from the base and tag the bag with your hand as you go by. Again the idea is to give the fielder very little to tag.

But remember, at your level, the popup slide is best. And once more, before you slide in a game, *practice*!

The worst has happened! I'm caught off base! Help! If you're caught off base and know you can't get back (and there's no runner directly ahead of you), your best bet is to head straight for the next base. Maybe the fielders will mishandle the ball.

If you're caught off second or third with a runner behind you, make the fielders work to put you out. The more times the fielders have to throw the ball, the more likely they'll throw it away. And, even if you're finally put out, you may have been able to give the other runners time to move up a base.

If you're caught off base, try to make the fielders throw the ball as much as possible during a rundown play. The more they handle it, the better your chances that someone will throw the ball away or that someone will miss catching it.

Tips from great baserunners

Vince Coleman of the St. Louis Cardinals is one of the top base stealers in major league history. He's had three seasons with more than 100 stolen bases. In 1989 Vince set a new record by stealing fifty straight bases before being caught. "Obviously the faster you run the better your chance to reach the next base safely," Coleman says. You should always give it your best effort. Never trot or lope on the bases when the ball is in play. Once you're sure you're heading for a base, *run!* "Most of the time in running the bases, you're your own best coach. In your mind, you know how many outs there are and how well the fielder can throw. In running to second on a hit to left field or center field, you should be able to see the play developing in front of you and know if you can try for third. If the ball is hit to right field, take a quick glance at the play.

"When you're heading for third on a ball hit to the outfield, the play is behind you and looking back will only slow you down so watch the third base coach. He'll tell you whether to slide, stay up, or keep running.

"Never let a pitcher intimidate you into cutting down your lead," Coleman tells young runners. "You should take the maximum amount of distance that you can and still get back to the base on a pickoff attempt.

"Watch the pitcher's knee. The knee's the key. Once his knee moves toward the plate, he must pitch and cannot try to pick you off. When his knee goes home, you go to second.

"The best reason to use a popup slide is that you can get quickly to your feet and run to the next base," Vince says. "When I was 10 years old and just learning, I got a lot of 'strawberries' (scrapes) learning a popup slide. Everybody thought it was cute. It hurt, but I practiced until I got it right.

"Practice the popup until you've mastered it. When you're about 15 or so, you can try hook slides and hand-tags."

Coleman is the second great basestealer to play left field for the Cardinals. Lou Brock put in nineteen major league seasons and stole 938 bases, while running opponents ragged and himself into the Hall of Fame.

"Before you do anything," Brock, who had a lifetime batting average of .293, says, "you've got to get to first base. Work on getting out of the batter's box *fast*. After you hit the ball, don't stand there and admire it. Get down to first in a hurry!

"Run with intensity. Remember, the sight of you storming down the basepath can force errors—and that means extra bases."

Brock points out that you should "practice rounding the bases. Try and touch the inside corner of the bag with your left foot as you round the base." That technique helped him score 1,610 runs during his major league career.

Brett Butler of the San Francisco Giants is one of the game's best bunters.

CHAPTER 4

Bunting

Learning to bunt is not the most important skill for you to learn right now. In fact some leagues for players your age don't even allow players to bunt.

While a bunt can occasionally be used to surprise a defense and get a hit, it's most commonly used as a "sacrifice" with none or one out. The batter gives up an out in order to advance a runner or runners into scoring position. A sacrifice can be very important late in a close game.

How do you make a good sacrifice bunt? As the pitcher winds, square around by bringing your back foot forward to almost even with your front foot. At the same time bring the bat around to even with your armpits, with the barrel end slightly higher than the handle. The bat angle is important, so remember, keep the barrel up. Slide your back hand up the bat to the barrel to a point even with the label. Grip the bat there, with your thumb on top and your crooked index finger on the bottom.

Bend your knees slightly. If the pitch is low, bend your knees further.

Remember, your bat is even with your armpits, so don't go for any pitch higher than that. It's a ball and even if you bunt it, you'll pop it up. As a strike comes in, keep the bat barrel up, dropping both of your hands to lower the bat.

Lay the fat part of the bat in front of the ball, and let the ball hit it. Don't punch at the pitch. Some instructors say, "Lay the bat on the top of the ball" to make sure the bunt goes on the ground. That's a little tricky and can result in missing the ball completely. If you start with your bat barrel higher than the handle, you'll normally be bringing the bat down to meet the pitch anyway, and the bunt should go safely on the ground.

Should I sacrifice bunt toward first base or third? With some practice you can learn to angle your bat toward first or third base to control the direction the bunt will take.

With a runner on first base it's best to bunt down the first base line because it will be a little harder for the first baseman to make a play on the runner going to second. With a runner on second you want to force the third baseman to come in and make the play on the ball (instead of waiting at third to make a putout), so bunt toward him.

How should I bunt to get a hit? Surprise is your best weapon. The technique is the same, but don't square around so soon. You want to keep the fielders back expecting you to swing. Bunting away from the pitcher down a foul line toward the farthest fielder (first or third baseman) is your second best weapon.

Some players, particularly lefthanded batters, learn to "drag bunt." On these, they don't square around, but are already moving toward first base as they bunt the ball. The idea is to bunt the ball hard enough between the pitcher's mound and the base line so that it rolls past the pitcher before he can field it. At the same time, it must be bunted soft enough that by the time the infielder gets to it, the runner is already on first.

As you can imagine, a drag bunt is a very difficult

When bunting, the safest thing to do is cradle the barrel of the bat between your index finger and thumb, but make sure your thumb is on top of the bat and not wrapped around it.

play to execute properly and takes a tremendous amount of practice. Learn to make an ordinary sacrifice correctly first before you even think about drag bunts.

Any other tips on bunting? Try devoting a whole practice at bat to bunts. The secret to bunting well is the same as the secret to doing anything else well—practice!

A righthanded batter should keep the bat back near the catcher to push a bunt toward first base.

To pull a bunt toward third base, your bat should be out over the plate and away from the catcher.

PART 2

The Defense

Boston's Roger Clemens has a classic pitching delivery, driving toward home plate with tremendous thrust from his legs.

CHAPTER 5

Pitching

Baseball managers, coaches, and players have argued for years about the importance of pitching. Some have said it's as much as "75 percent of baseball." Some have said less. But almost everyone agrees that the pitcher's performance is the single most important factor in winning or losing. That's why—when the game is over—it isn't the player with a "game-winning" home run or the fellow with a "game-saving" catch who gets credit for a "W" in the box score. It's a pitcher.

And the opposing team's pitcher gets an "L."

Being your team's pitcher is a big responsibility, and you'll want to give it your best effort.

Getting Ready and Staying Fit

A pitcher needs strong legs; that's where his power comes from when he throws. Most major league pitching coaches have their pitchers do a lot of running when they're not on the mound.

Weight lifting is also becoming common, so long as it's used in combination with stretching exercises to preserve flexibility.

Of course, you throw with your arm. As a pitcher, your arm is your most valuable possession, so you must protect it.

Always make sure your arm is properly loosened with stretching exercises before you throw. Then warm up gradually, throwing easily at first. Throw hard only when you're completely heated.

Between innings protect your arm from cooling off by wearing a jacket on the bench. After a game, repeat your stretching exercises to help avoid stiffness.

Don't wear out your young arm by throwing more pitches than it's ready for. Most youth leagues have rules about how many innings a youngster can pitch during a week.

Most important of all: use proper mechanics when throwing to reduce the strain on your arm, and stay away from pitches like curves that put extra strain on your elbow.

Never pitch if your arm is sore.

Control: The Secret of Success

What's the most important thing to becoming a good pitcher? Control. No matter how hard you throw or how well you know the hitters, you can't accomplish anything until you put the ball over the plate.

Practice is the key. At first you may not see a lot of improvement, but stay at it. Concentrate on where you're throwing. Always aim at a target.

But don't "aim the ball." That's when a pitcher abandons his natural motion or doesn't throw hard in order to get the ball over the plate. It's one of the worst things you can do. Not only is it unlikely to work because you'd be throwing unnaturally, but even if you finally got the ball over, a batter can crush it. As your control improves you'll start hitting those corners.

You can practice at home. All you need is space to throw, a wall that you're allowed to throw against and an old baseball. Also make certain that a pitch a little off-line isn't going to go through a window.

Mark off a strike zone on the wall and measure to a spot sixty feet away. (If your league uses a shorter distance, measure that instead.) Remember, the strike zone is the area from the batter's armpits to his knees and the width of the plate across.

Always throw a baseball. Throwing a lighter ball like a tennis ball won't help nearly as much.

Although you'd like to have steady improvement, sometimes you'll seem to slip back a bit and your control won't be as good as it was a few days or weeks before. The most common cause is that you've gone away from your normal motion. Some pitchers have had themselves videotaped when they were going well so they could study their own motion if they started having problems.

On the other hand, your body is growing right now and you may have to make adjustments. For example, let's say your stride was exactly three feet last year. This year you're three inches taller. You should lengthen your stride to keep the "same" motion.

One more tip: don't get discouraged if you can't throw strikes right away. If you're doing everything right, your control will improve sooner or later. Practice!

What is the correct pitching motion? Everyone's different so there's no one perfect pitching motion. It's important to use a motion that's comfortable, keeps you balanced, and, most important, doesn't put unnecessary strain on your arm. Below is a "generic" pitching motion (for a righthanded thrower), but you may well find that some adjustments work for you.

Let's start with the first pitch of a game. There's no one on base:

Stance. Face the batter, shoulders level, weight forward. Put your right foot on the rubber with the toe of your shoe over the edge and angled slightly toward third base. Your left foot is back a few inches. While taking the sign, hold the ball behind your right thigh to hide it from the batter.

Pump. Lean forward. Swing your arms back. Shift your weight to your left foot and straighten up. Bring your arms forward and up, your hands brushing past your hips. Join your hands above your head, hiding the ball from the batter with your glove.

Pivot. Slide your right foot forward into the hole on the batter's side of the rubber. Turn your body to the right. Shift your weight to your right foot. Bring your throwing arm back and at the same time lift your left leg up and to the right so that you're looking at your target over your left shoulder. Don't bring that leg up too far; it can throw you off balance.

Stride. Step straight at the batter with your left leg. Your foot should hit the ground flat—not heelfirst—with your toe aimed at the plate. Push off the rubber with your right leg, putting your body behind the pitch, as you bring your right arm up and over. This push is where most of your power comes from and why pitchers need strong legs.

Follow-through. Let the force of your throw pull you around. Don't make a sudden stop; you could hurt your arm. Your right foot will actually end up slightly forward of your left. Now square around to become a fielder and bring your glove up to be ready.

Can I use the same motion with men on base? No. The runners will steal you blind. With runners on base, pitch from a stretch.

When you begin your motion, bring your arms forward until they meet above your head.

Your right foot then slides to the right side of the rubber and the weight is now on your back leg.

Next, step toward the batter pushing off the rubber and throwing toward the plate.

Finally, your arm should follow through and end by your left hip.

Stance. Face third base, but keep your left shoulder back a little toward first base. Right foot on the inside of the rubber. Weight on your right foot. Left foot parallel to the right and comfortably forward with the toe pointing slightly toward the plate. Hands together at the waist. You can turn your head to check the runner on first, but you must hold your body still or the umpire can call a balk and send the runner to second.

Pump. You can stretch your arms by lifting them above your head and bringing them back down to your waist. However, the rules say you must come to a complete stop before delivering or it's a balk. Because of this, many pitchers skip a stretch.

From this point on, your motion is the same as your normal windup except it's a good idea to avoid lifting your left leg very high—runners can get too good a start. A quick step along the ground is best.

What is a balk? Usually balks aren't called too often at your level, but you should know about them. The balk rule was written to protect baserunners. Basically, it says, if you make a move toward home, you must throw there; if you move toward first, you must throw there. You can fake toward second or third with no penalty. A lot of major league balks are called when umpires think the pitcher has moved his knee toward the plate and then thrown to first. Another part of the balk rule states that you must come to a full stop after taking a stretch. This is because some pitchers used to hide their move to first with their stretch move.

How do you know when to throw to a base to pick the runner off? At the major league level, pitchers don't pick off a lot of runners. The runners are too smart. Mostly pitchers throw to a base to force a runner to shorten his lead so he can't steal. That's important. Most teams have signs so the catcher or fielder can tell the pitcher to throw to a base, but a lot of it he'll do on his own. If he thinks the runner is leading off too far, he'll throw to first.

By the way, the key is not how hard you throw but how quick, so practice making quick, accurate pickoff throws.

If a curve might hurt my arm, what can I throw besides a fastball? The first thing to ask yourself is how good is your fastball? If at your age you can get the good hitters out with fastballs, there's no reason to go to any other pitch. In fact, you'd be doing the batters a big favor by slowing down for another kind of pitch. The fastball is your best friend.

How do I hold a fastball? Your thumb on the bottom and your first two fingers on top. Don't grip the ball too far back in your hand as that will reduce speed. When you throw, the ball should roll off the tips of your first two fingers.

Should I hold the ball with the seams or across them? At your level, many youngsters must hold the ball with their whole hand to control it. Even if your hand is big enough to give you a choice, there's no right answer. Some pitchers prefer one way; some the other. But the pitch will behave differently depending on which way you hold it. Experiment with both grips until you know which feels better

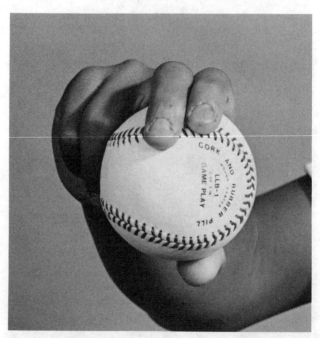

To throw a fastball, place your thumb on the bottom of the ball and your index and middle fingers on the top.

in your hand and what the pitch will do. The important thing is to have a grip that feels comfortable.

If I want to change speeds, what do I do? Again it may depend on the size of your hand. A simple way to slow your pitch while still using your fastball motion is to hold the ball farther back in your hand so that more of your palm touches the ball. The success of a slower pitch depends on fooling the batter and getting him out in front with his swing. If the batters are having trouble getting around on your fastball, throwing them changeups just makes it easier for them.

What about screwballs, sliders, and other such pitches? This book will not teach you any pitches that involve twisting your elbow. In a few years you'll be ready for those pitches. Not now. Another problem is that some pitches, like the famous split-finger fastball, require longer fingers than most players your age have. And finally, any time spent practicing extra pitches now takes time away from your main concern at this stage: learning control.

You can change the speed of your pitches simply by holding the ball farther back in the palm of your hand. You would throw this pitch with the same motion and arm speed as you would a fastball.

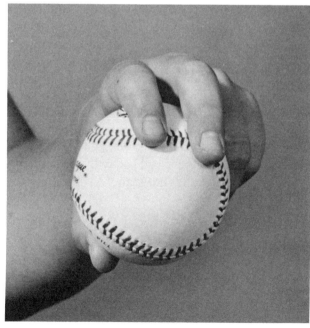

Some pitchers prefer to hold the ball with the seams while other pitchers prefer holding it against the seams. It's best to experiment to see which way feels better to you and what type of movement you can obtain on your pitches.

Why do pitchers wear such large gloves? One reason is to help them hide the ball better from the batter, but the main reason is that the ball can come back past the mound pretty fast. Sometimes there's only enough time to throw up your hand to knock the ball down and a large glove helps.

What about fielding? It's important. As soon as you turn that ball loose, you become an infielder. The first thing is to be in a proper fielding position. Your follow-through (discussed above) should leave you squared toward the plate and ready to break left or right.

With a runner on base, be alert. On a ball hit back to you or a bunt that you field, your catcher will tell you whether to throw to first or to try to cut the baserunner down.

On any ball hit past you to the first base side of the infield, you should break for first. Naturally, if the first baseman is already there or if he's running to make the putout himself, you must get out of his way.

Another thing to remember, don't run straight to the bag. Head for a spot on the baseline a couple of feet toward home so you can "belly out" and take a throw while running up the line instead of away from the fielder. Step on the inside corner of the bag and then turn toward second base.

Major league pitchers almost never catch pop-ups—even those that come down right on the mound. They're surrounded by talented infielders. But on your level, you might be the best fielder out there. Ask your coach how he wants it handled.

On a wild pitch or a passed ball with runners on second or third, don't just stand on the mound shaking your head. Cover the plate!

If your catcher is involved in a rundown between third and home, you cover home by taking a position just a step up the third base line.

On a play involving a throw home from the outfield, you should take a position about ten feet behind the catcher as a backup in case of an overthrow.

As soon as you release the ball you become a fielder. You must prepare yourself for any balls hit back up the middle.

Tips from the mound

Rick Sutcliffe of the Chicago Cubs won the National League's Cy Young Award in 1984 with a 16-1 record. With well over 100 major league victories, Sutcliffe is one of the top righthanders in baseball (although he still has a long way to go to match the "original" Cy Young who earned 511 victories).

Rick advises waiting until you're a senior in high school before you start working on curves. "And then, most important," he says, "find someone who has the ability to teach you to throw a curve properly. Throwing it incorrectly can damage your arm even when you're older."

And that brings up Sutcliffe's most important advice to all young players: "A lot of kids do the things they do well rather than work on the things they struggle with. Work on the things you have trouble with. If you're a good hitter and have trouble in the field, take a lot of groundballs. If you have trouble hitting, the only way to improve is get out there and hit. If you need to work on your control, do it."

Tom Seaver, who retired after the 1986 season with 311 wins, won three Cy Young Awards during his twenty-year career. In five different seasons, he won 20 or more games. "Tom Terrific" is expected to be a shoo-in for the Hall of Fame as soon as he's eligible. When Tom was growing up in Fresno, California, he was smaller than most boys his age and couldn't throw fast. "Fortunately," he says, "it was the best thing to ever happen to me because I used to have to set up my fastball." Tom learned to pitch with his head, using good control.

After high school Tom joined the Marines. When he came back, he was thirty-five pounds heavier and four inches taller. He had "velocity for the first time and "I really didn't know how to control it. I was so much stronger physically that my rhythm and timing were very bad because I could do things so much quicker. I had to learn to pitch all over again."

Nolan Ryan is baseball's all-time strike-out leader with more than 5,000 whiffs to his credit. Perhaps no one has thrown so fast for so many seasons. When the "Ryan Express" is working, he's often unhittable. In fact he's thrown an unbelievable six no-hitters at major league batters. Nolan, who throws as fast as any man who ever pitched, learned an important lesson one day pitching to slugger Reggie Jackson: "I got a two-strike count on Jackson. I wanted to get him on three straight fastballs." Ryan threw his third pitch as hard as he'd ever thrown a ball in his life. "I wanted to blow it by him," he admits. Instead, he blew out his own arm. "There was no pain in my arm but it felt like a rubber band expanding." Ryan missed three weeks with a strained right elbow and went on to have one of his few poor seasons.

Now he counsels against overthrowing. "The tendency of a fastball pitcher is to muscle up and do what he needs to do. He winds up lunging and losing his rhythm to muscle the ball in there. Everybody has limits. You just have to learn what the limits are and deal with them accordingly. I know the kind of pitcher I am and I'd be defeating my purposes if I tried to 'overthrow' myself."

Bob Gibson earned his plaque in the Hall of Fame with 251 victories for the St. Louis Cardinals. One of baseball's toughest competitors, he broke his leg during the 1967 season, yet came back to win three games in the World Series that year. Bob, a Hall of Famer, explains why a pitcher has to use all of the plate: "The inside part of the plate already belongs to the hitter, so you throw inside some of the time to keep him from leaning out and taking the outside." In other words, if the batter *knows* you're going to throw every pitch for the outside corner, he'll adjust. Keep him guessing.

Pittsburgh's Doug Drabek is another outstanding National League pitcher. The stylish Texan has been the Pirates "ace" since 1987, earning a reputation as a tough competitor who "keeps his team in the game" until the late innings.

Doug tells young pitchers: "You want to build

up your legs. The stronger your legs are, the harder you can throw. At the major league level we do a lot of running and even lift weights. Nolan Ryan is a great example of someone who really works with weights. You won't lose flexibility if you do proper stretching exercises before and after. But running is the most common exercise. Another good one is jumping rope. We did a lot of that in college."

Drabek suggests, "Always do stretching exercises to loosen your arm before you pick up a baseball. When you start in throwing, start slow and easy. Then gradually build up.

"Don't throw off a mound every day, but throw some every day. We throw every day for fifteen minutes—about sixty pitches—to loosen our arms. You shouldn't throw that much; probably about forty pitches is plenty. The day after I pitch in a game, I'll be a little stiff and sore, but I'll throw a little until my arm gets loose and then quit.

"Always throw with a good follow-through. Stopping short can damage your arm.

"Cold is an enemy. In cool weather, always wear a long-sleeve shirt that covers the elbow. Between innings put on a jacket. Even on hot days I'll wear a light jacket between innings. After you're finished throwing, do your stretching exercises.

"Listen to your arm," Drabek says. "For that matter, to your whole body. If something hurts beyond normal stiffness, or if it keeps hurting after you should be loose, stop and tell your coach. Never throw hard if your arm hurts. Sure you want to go out there and do well, but taking a chance like that won't help your team, and it could do permanent damage to your arm."

Drabek explains how to improve your control:

Doug Drabek of the Pittsburgh Pirates.

Paul Assenmacher of the Chicago Cubs.

"Control is good concentration on the mitt. You've seen major league pitchers who turn their heads away before throwing, but they're older guys who've had a long time to learn how to pitch. At your level, keep your eye on that catcher's mitt. Even today, when I'm throwing on the sidelines, I concentrate on throwing strikes down the middle. If you can hit the catcher's mitt, you can worry about the corners by simply having the catcher move a little left or right."

Drabek says: "It's good to experiment with different motions at first. Some pitchers throw over the top; some throw three-quarters. Some have a high leg kick. Others not so high. Some grip the ball across the seams; others prefer a grip with the seams. You want to establish a motion that's comfortable for you—one that you can stay balanced with. Once you've found it, throw every pitch with that motion. You're training your body to do exactly what it must do to throw strikes."

"Don't throw curves," says Drabek. "I saw a lot of guys hurt their arms trying to throw curves when I was your age. Of course, it's really up to you, your parents, and your coach. But I would stay away from any pitch that involves twisting your elbow. If you want a pitch other than a fastball, throw a changeup or a sinker."

Lefty Paul Assenmacher of the Cubs has never been a big winner in his five major league seasons. His top victory total was 8 in 1988. His value to his team isn't reflected in his win-loss stats. Assenmacher is a specialist—a middle reliever. His job is to come to the rescue of a starting pitcher, hold the opposition for a few innings, and then turn the game over to a "closer." When all goes well, the starter gets the win, the closer gets a "save," and Paul gets the satisfaction of knowing he did a tough job well. A reliever needs even better control than a starting pitcher because he often comes into a game with runners already on the bases. "Even if you're throwing rocks at a tree," Paul, "control comes from practice."

Paul agrees that young pitchers should avoid curves, but adds, "As a kid growing up I never had a good fastball so I started throwing curves about seventh grade. But other fellows my age who threw curves, by the time they got to high school, they couldn't pitch any more. I was lucky! Wait until your arm develops."

On the subject of putting your body behind the throw, Assenmacher says: "Look at Nolan Ryan. He's over 40 years old and has been throwing hard in the majors for more than twenty years. He still throws over ninety-miles-per-hour. Why? Because he has perfect mechanics. He gets the maximum ability out of his body by pushing off with his legs and keeping the strain off his arm."

Be sure to end up in a position to field a ball hit back to you. "Give yourself a chance to field anything back through the middle," Assenmacher says. "There's a gap between the shortstop and the second baseman for you to fill. Be ready. All you've got to do most of the time is knock the ball down. Pitchers can help themselves in a lot of ballgames by fielding their positions."

Luis Salazar of the Chicago Cubs is one of the game's most versatile players.

CHAPTER 6

Playing the Infield

Quickness, agility, a strong arm and sure hands are all needed to play second base, shortstop, or third base. The first three are useful in a first baseman too, but many managers prefer to have a big target at first base and will give up a little quickness, agility and arm strength so long as their big guy can catch anything the other infielders throw at him. Besides sure hands, another thing all four infielders had better have in common is a taste for action. A lot happens in the infield. And it happens *fast*!

Be ready.

As the pitcher is about to deliver, crouch with your feet spread comfortably apart, your weight evenly distributed, your knees slightly bent. Lean forward slightly. Hold your hands down low, just in front of your knees.

Follow the pitch. When it's halfway to the plate, be up on the balls of your feet, ready to move in any direction.

Fielding groundballs

If the ball is hit on the ground in your direction, try to get in front of it. Naturally you want to field it with your glove, but should it take a bad hop you can still block it with your body.

Keep your hands away from your knees. Many a grounder has been booted because the fielder bumped his glove with his knee. Field the ball out in front. Watch the ball all the way and use two hands. Look the ball right into the pocket of your glove and fold your throwing hand over it. Under no circumstances should you turn your head away from a bouncing ball. That last hop may not be right where you expect it.

If at all possible move in on the ball. That way you're in control. You decide which bounce to field the ball on. Another advantage is that you'll have extra time to throw out the runner.

When you move back, you're "letting the ball play you." Yes, there are times when this is all you can do, but most of the time it's up to you to take charge.

For balls hit only slightly to your left or right, use a side shuffle step with no crossover step, but when the ball is well away from you, push off with the foot nearest where you want to be and then cross over with your other leg. Try to get to the spot before the ball does so you can square around and face the ball.

It may sometimes be necessary to be right in the baseline to field the ball. You, the fielder, have a right to be there; it's up to the baserunner to avoid you.

Throwing

Fielding the ball is only half the job. Now you have to throw somebody out.

Pitchers wind up; infielders don't have time.

You should be able to throw to the base with no more than a single step out of the position in which you caught the ball. Plant your rear foot. Step toward the base.

If there's time, straighten up and throw overhand. Your throw will be more accurate and have more on it. If it's going to be a close play, you may have to throw sidearm out of a crouch. Practice both throws.

Try to use a four-seam grip. That's just what it sounds like. Your thumb, index, and middle finger are touching all four seams of the baseball. The ball will carry better than on a two-seam grip.

Think. Know where you're going to throw before you catch the ball. Always know the score, how many outs there are, and how many men are on base. Never make a long throw when a short one will do better. For example, with a runner on first, you may have a shorter, quicker throw to second for a forceout than to throw across the diamond to first.

When throwing for a forceout aim above the fielder's waist so he can catch the ball easily. When throwing for a tagout aim below his waist so he won't have far to bend to apply the tag.

If you can make the putout by running to the bag yourself and not throwing, do it, unless you're going for a double play and the first out must be made quickly. But be sure you can make the play.

When you're close to the bag but still have to throw, it's best to make an underhand toss.

Pop flies

Besides fielding grounders infielders get a lot of action on pop flies.

Infielders sometimes miss easy pop flies when they let the ball play them. They drift with the fly. Learn to judge where the ball is going to come down and then get to that spot as quickly as you can.

And always use two hands.

Catch popups with your arms over your head and your hands in front of your face so you can watch the ball coming down over the top of your glove. This way you can watch every moment of the flight and you're ready to make a quick throw if necessary. Another advantage is that you can use your glove to block out bright sunlight.

If you're wearing flip-down sunglasses, tap them down as soon as the ball is hit, even if the sun isn't out. The glasses will help you see the ball against a gray sky. Moreover, the sun might suddenly appear. On any infield popup, let the other infielders know if you intend to catch it by shouting, "I've got it!" *Loudly*. And *many* times. When you're going back to catch flyballs, shout to the outfielders to prevent a collision. Let the outfielder catch the ball if he calls for it. It's easier to catch a ball coming toward it.

Here's something first and third basemen should be aware of. A foul pop over near the stands will spin in such a way that it will come back toward the

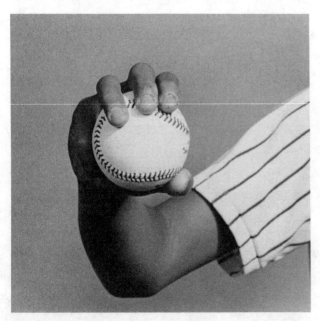

When you throw the ball in the infield, always use a four-seam grip.

playing field. Don't give up on a ball that looks at first like it's going to be just out of reach.

While the ball is coming down, you should be thinking of what is likely to happen after you catch it. Is there a runner on third? Could he tag up and try to score? Are there runners who might be caught off base?

You should also know the Infield Fly Rule. This applies when there are fewer than two out and first and second base or first, second and third are occupied. The batter hits a pop fly that an infielder can catch while facing the infield. The umpire immediately calls the batter out even if the fielder drops the ball. This is so the infielder can't intentionally muff the ball and set up a double play on the runners.

Relays and cutoffs

When the ball is hit to the outfield, the fielder—usually the one nearest the play or the one with the best arm—goes out to serve as the relay man.

Meanwhile the remaining infielder on the side the throw is coming in on, lines himself up between the base and the relay man. For example, there's a runner on second and the ball is hit deep to right.

The second baseman goes out to relay the throw; the first baseman lines himself up between the second baseman and home plate. The outfielder throws to the second baseman, who throws for the plate. If there's going to be a play at the plate, the first baseman can let the throw go through to the catcher, but if the runner rounds third and stops, the first baseman can cut off the throw and whip it to third to catch the runner. More often the runner from second will have home plate made; then the first baseman can cut off the throw and throw to the shortstop at second base to keep the runner from advancing past first.

Words of wisdom

Luis Salazar of the Cubs is one of baseball's most versatile players. The native of Venezuela has played every position but catcher in his eleven major league seasons.

His advice for any infielder: "Prepare yourself before the game. Know who's going to pitch, and think about the hitters on the other team."

And once the game starts, "Be alert!"

Keith Hernandez of the Cleveland Indians is one of the greatest fielding first baseman ever.
He's won eleven Gold Glove Awards during his career.

CHAPTER 7

Playing First Base

Where does the first baseman normally stand? Believe it or not, a hundred years ago first basemen stood with one foot on the bag *all the time*. The first first baseman to realize he could field many more groundballs by playing away from the bag was Charles Comiskey in the 1880s. That name may sound familiar to you. Comiskey Park, the home of the Chicago White Sox, was named for the old first baseman who founded the team.

In normal fielding position, you should be about eight feet from the foul line and about fifteen feet behind the base. Play closer to second base for righthanded hitters than for lefthanded hitters.

Know your opposing hitters and whether or not they have speed. When a slower runner is at bat, you can play a little deeper than the normal fifteen feet.

What is the first baseman's main job? What a first baseman does most often is catch throws from the other fielders. Therefore you should practice catching throws every chance you get. And not just the easy ones. You should practice taking wide throws, high throws, and throws in the dirt until you feel confident about taking any throw. Then practice some more.

A first baseman wears a special glove so he can catch those difficult throws with one hand. If you have to really stretch out, a one-hand grab may be the only way you can reach the ball. But, just because you *can* catch with one hand, that doesn't mean you *should* catch with one hand. The best rule is: if you can reach it with two hands, *use* two hands. As the ball goes into your glove, fold your other hand over top of it to keep it from popping loose.

If you can't catch a bad throw, block it. The runner may get one base, but if the ball gets past you he'll probably get two.

As soon as a ball is hit to another infielder, run to first base as fast as you can. Don't saunter to the bag. The infielder wants a stationary target when he throws. It's much harder to hit a moving target. Even if the runner is slow as molasses, run to the bag as quickly as you can. When an infielder fields the ball and then has to break his rhythm to wait for you, he's very likely to make a bad throw.

When you get to the bag, touch it with one foot. Then straddle it so you can shift in either direction and still keep one foot on the bag.

Expect a bad throw. That way you'll be ready when you get one.

When a throw is straight to you, simply step forward with your left foot and catch it.

On a throw to the inside (down the base line toward home), you step in that direction keeping your body toward the throw and your toe on the bag. Sometimes such throws are right into the runner. Make your stretch in fair territory; the rules say the runner must stay to the outside of the base line so if you stay fair you'll avoid a collision.

On a throw slightly toward the outside you can take an easy step right with your right foot and bring your left foot onto the bag. If the throw is very wide to the outside, you keep your right toe on the bag, reach across your body and catch backhand.

How should I handle throws in the dirt? One of the hardest throws to take is one that's low. You have to judge this. If you can stretch forward and catch the ball before it bounces, do so. If you see it's going to bounce close in front of you, the best way to handle it (if you have time) is to step *behind* the base, keep your right toe on the bag, and field the throw on the hop. Naturally you shouldn't do this on a close play because the runner will run right over you.

Unless you can't reach the throw any other way, don't move your toe from the bag because it's hard to get back in time to put the runner out. But make sure you can reach and catch the ball. It's better to come off the bag to make the catch (and allow the runner to be safe at first) than to stretch and not reach the ball (and allow the runner to go all the way to second).

Just as you practice catching the ball, practice your footwork until you don't even have to think about it.

What's the hardest throw for a first baseman? The hardest throw a righthanded first baseman must make is to second base. For that reason many first basemen are lefthanded throwers.

Let's look at the problem a righthanded thrower encounters. When he fields a grounder with a runner on first and wants to throw to second for a forceout, he must turn all the way around to throw. This takes precious time and the runner may be safe. With a little practice, you'll learn if you have time to make this difficult play. Sometimes it may be better to take the easier out at first. Naturally, when there are already two outs, it's almost always best to take the out at first base.

To throw to second, pivot on your right foot, stepping toward second and bringing your body around to make a hard, straight throw.

Any other tips? Whether you throw lefthanded or righthanded, try to avoid fielding the ball at the same depth as the baseline between first and second. When you are about to throw, you'll probably find the baserunner in the way between you and the fielder covering second. If you charge the ball, you'll improve the angle of your throw as well as give yourself more time to make the play.

And don't forget to hustle back to first base for a return throw. The 3-6-3 double play is one of the prettiest in baseball.

What if I field the ball and have to throw to first? A common play for a first baseman is to field a ball to his right and then throw to the pitcher covering first. Here a righthander has an advantage on an overhand throw. Sometimes you'll still be close enough to the base that an underhand toss would be best. Regardless of the kind of throw you make, remember, the pitcher is moving fast and you must lead him. Try to throw the ball so that he gets it just before he steps on the base. Put it to him shoulder-high; it will be very hard for him to bend for a low throw while running.

You, the pitcher, and the second baseman should always huddle before the pitch in a bunt situation, so all of you know who will field the ball and who will cover first.

How do I hold a runner at first? Let's say you throw lefthanded. When you're holding a runner on first you have your right foot on the inside corner of the base. And your left foot is at an angle. That way you squarely face the pitcher—the guy you're working with.

Now you're in a good position to get a good view of both the pitcher and the batter. You need that at all times. You've got to see the batter. Never get in a position where you block him out.

You face the pitcher at about a forty-five degree angle to the foul line.

Give the pitcher a good target with your glove low, near the base so when you do get the ball you can quickly put it on the runner. The pitcher has to throw low and toward the base. Your glove is the target.

If the pitcher throws to you, you must catch the ball first! A pickoff that gets past you is almost certainly going to allow the runner to run to second.

If the pitcher makes a terrible throw that an octopus couldn't catch, don't stand there and glare at him. Get after that ball!

Once you've caught the ball, bring it down in your glove to your right between the runner and the bag. Here it doesn't matter whether you throw left or right; always tag down and to your right. Down because on any close play the runner will be sliding back to the base; to your right because if you turn left you can't watch to see if the runner has taken off for second.

Your team may have a special pickoff play or two with the pitcher or catcher. When you get the sign, you "sell" the play by moving back to your normal fielding position as though you don't care if the runner takes a long lead. At the signal, usually a shout or on a count, you dash for first and the

Two important plays a first baseman must master: holding a runner on base and putting the tag on a runner returning to the base during a pickoff attempt.

all times. You've got to see the batter. Never get in a position where you block him out.

You face the pitcher at about a forty-five degree angle to the foul line.

Give the pitcher a good target with your glove low, near the base so when you do get the ball you can quickly put it on the runner. The pitcher has to throw low and toward the base. Your glove is the target.

If the pitcher throws to you, you must catch the ball first! A pickoff that gets past you is almost certainly going to allow the runner to run to second. If the pitcher makes a terrible throw that an octopus couldn't catch, don't stand there and glare at him. Get after that ball!

Once you've caught the ball, bring it down in your glove to your right between the runner and the bag. Here it doesn't matter whether you throw left or right; always tag down and to your right. Down because on any close play the runner will be sliding back to the base; to your right because if you turn left you can't watch to see if the runner has taken off for second.

Your team may have a special pickoff play or two with the pitcher or catcher. When you get the sign, you "sell" the play by moving back to your normal fielding position as though you don't care if the runner takes a long lead. At the signal, usually a shout or on a count, you dash for first and the thrower fires the ball toward the base before you are there. Obviously, it's your job to make it there in time.

Any other tips? Remember, the pitcher wants to fool the runner into thinking he's not going to try a pickoff. Don't let him fool *you*. Watch your pitcher carefully. After you've worked with him for a while, you should be able to tell when he's coming over.

If he pitches to the plate, take a sideways hop-step or two back toward your normal fielding position to get ready for a ball hit down to you.

A gold glover's advice

Keith Hernandez, who starred with the St. Louis Cardinals and New York Mets, has been called the best fielding first baseman ever. His eleven straight Gold Gloves (1978 through 1988) are far more than any other first sacker has ever garnered.

"First base is, what, one quarter of the infield?" he says. "Okay, my responsibility is one quarter of the infield."

Keith says he owes much of his fielding ability to his father, who coached him as a boy. "He wouldn't let us hit unless we worked on our fielding. By the time I got to Little League I knew my position."

He stresses keeping his glove low to the ground as the ball is pitched. "From the time I was 7, when my father taught me, I always had my glove down. One time I had a bullet hit at me by Vince Coleman that I literally had no time to react to. The ball was there in my glove; my glove was like a magnet to the ball."

CHAPTER 8

Playing Second Base

Do I need a powerful arm to play second? Arm power isn't the first requirement. Compared to the long throws the shortstop and third baseman must make, most of the second baseman's throws are short—ninety feet or less. Accuracy and getting the ball away quickly are more important than having a "cannon" for an arm.

What are the main qualities I need? The ability to throw quickly and accurately.

Quick feet are also important. A second baseman may have to race in for a slow hit on one play, dash out into short right field on the next, and reach a ball bounding over second base on the third play. And of course he has to get out of the way of a runner in a double play.

Courage is crucial. You must be willing to stand there on a tag play and concentrate on your throw to first on the double play. You can't be "gun shy" of the runner running at you full tilt.

Should I throw to first sidearmed on a slow grounder? Often that's the only way the play can be made, so practice it. Naturally, if there's time, you should straighten up and make an overhand throw. Remember, the quicker you can get to the ball, the more time you'll have to make your throw.

On a pop fly down the first base line, whose ball is it? If the outfielder calls for it, it's his because he has a better view of the play. Your back is to the infield, and you probably can't know what the baserunners might be doing. On the other hand, you have a better angle in judging the flight of the ball than the first baseman, so if it's a choice between the two of you, you should make the play. Be sure to tell him so by yelling "I've got it" loud and often.

How do I keep from running into the shortstop on a ball hit over second? Normally the shortstop takes the "inside track," heading for second base. If he can reach the ball, he'll be in a better position to throw to first than you. If he's going for a double play, he can step on the bag himself and throw. The second baseman usually races for a spot

When making the tag at second base, you straddle the bag with both feet and face the runner coming in from first base.

well behind second base. Although he may not be able to throw the runner out at first, he can keep a runner from scoring from second.

Where do I stand to make a tag at second? On a throw from the catcher, face first base but turned slightly toward the throw, straddle the bag with your feet out of the baseline. A throw from third base, right field or right-center is handled the same. On a throw from left field or left-center, you'll have to adjust so that you're not trying to catch a ball coming from behind you. It's much easier to shift your feet after you've caught the ball than to twist like a pretzel while waiting for the throw. If the throw is off-line, leave the base and go get it.

How do I apply the tag? Use two hands; the runner may try to kick the ball out of your glove. Bring the ball down between the runner and the base. Turn your hands so that the backs of your wrists are toward the runner. Let him slide into your

tag and put himself out; don't jab at him with the ball.

Keep your head down, eyes open, and watch the play; he may try to slide past the bag and reach back to tag it.

Who covers second on a steal attempt? Normally, of course, the second baseman will cover when a righthanded pull-hitter is at bat and the shortstop will cover when there's a lefthanded pull-hitter up. But if this is automatic, batters will be able to slap the ball through the hole left by the absent fielder.

You and the shortstop should decide between you who's covering before each play, considering the kind of batter and pitch. (Any batter is more likely to pull a slow pitch.) Obviously you can't yell back and forth, so one person should make the decision and give the sign.

A common sign is for the shortstop to hold his glove up to his face so only the second baseman can see his mouth. Mouth open means the shortstop covers. Mouth closed means the second baseman.

When should I look for the double play? Any time there are fewer than two outs and a runner on first base you should be alert to the possibility of getting two outs on any groundball. Remind the other infielders. But make sure that you get at least one out on a groundball. If the runner gets a good jump off first, he may have second base made before you get to the ball. Take the sure out at first base.

There's also a chance on a snagged line drive that you can throw to first before the runner can get back.

How do I start a double play on a groundball? Get to the ball as fast as you can, so you'll have more time to make your throw. You don't want to just fling the ball at the shortstop and hope he can handle it. If you've gone to your right, you should shovel a firm underhand toss to the shortstop. If you're not close to the bag, make a strong overhand throw. Either way, the shortstop should get the ball chest-high just *before* he gets to the base.

What should I do when I'm the pivot man?
When a groundball is hit to the third baseman or shortstop (with less than two outs and a runner on first), head for second base quickly. It's important that the fielder not have to wait for you. At the same time, keep your running under control. If the fielder hesitates, you may not be able to stop yourself from overrunning the base before the ball gets there. And if you're out of control, you won't be able to hop left or right for a bad throw.

Put your left foot on the bag and bend your knees. What you do next depends on the throw.

On a routine play you'll come across the bag toward third base with your right foot to get out of the baserunner's way. Then turn and throw to first.

If the throw is a little behind you, you'll step toward left field, actually moving away from first base. But then you get your momentum moving back toward first off your right foot. On a play like this, you may have to leap over a sliding baserunner.

If you're late getting to the bag—for example, on a hard-hit ball right at the fielder—you may have to step backward off the base toward right field. But it's still one step with your right foot, then step toward first with your left.

Concentrate on making a good throw. You're better taking a split second to set yourself up than to throw a "wounded duck" that (maybe) arcs to first.

When do I cover first base? If the first baseman isn't in position to get to the bag ahead of the runner, you may be elected. This usually happens on a bunt down the first base line. Both the pitcher and the first baseman are busy trying to field the ball, but who can the ball be thrown to if you don't cover first?

It's unusual for the second baseman to cover first when the first baseman fields a ball far to his right. Covering is the pitcher's job. But he may fall down or simply be slow. And you have already started to your left, so if the pitcher isn't going to make it and you can, go for it! On the other hand, if the pitcher is going to be there, get out of the way of the first baseman's throw.

Tips from a record-breaker

In 1990 Ryne Sandberg, the Chicago Cubs' great second baseman set new major league records for consecutive games by an infielder (excluding first basemen) without an error and for most chances accepted by a second baseman without an error. The National League's Most Valuable Player in 1984, Sandberg has been the league's Gold Glove second sacker seven times.

Ryne says: "The first rule for every infielder is *be ready*. Things happen fast in the infield. If you aren't awake to the situation and the possibilities, you can't help your team.

"I try to get in front of as many balls as possible," he says. "Go hard. That way, should you miss it with your glove, you may still knock it down with your body."

Some infielders like to catch popups with a "basket catch" where the arms are extended out in front as though holding a basket, but Sandberg says, "I don't like the basket catch because you can't follow the ball into your glove as well."

"Kids often ask about my glove," Sandberg says. "I use a smaller glove than the other infielders or outfielders because I often have to catch the ball and get rid of it in one motion. This is particularly true on double plays. If I used a bigger glove, I could have trouble finding the ball and digging it out.

"Kids should pick gloves they're comfortable with and that they can run with. Remember, a glove is an extension of your hand—not a big basket."

Acrobatic Ozzie Smith of the St. Louis Cardinals has been called the greatest fielding shortstop of all time. He has great speed and superb hands.

CHAPTER 9

Playing Shortstop

Is the shortstop usually the best defensive player? "Best" means a lot of different things. The catcher could be the "best" defender but be unable to play shortstop well. Much of what is true for the second baseman is true for the shortstop (and shortstops should read through that section, too). But there are some plays that are peculiar to shortstops. Shortstop is generally thought of as the most demanding position because it requires many different skills.

What skills are required? The shortstop must have a wide range in the field. That doesn't mean he has to be the fastest runner on the team, but he must be able to get a "jump" on the ball and move quickly to field it.

He must have sure hands. Over the course of a game, the shortstop will likely handle more batted balls than any other infielder or outfielder.

He must be agile. He has to be able to make the same kind of plays around second base that the second baseman makes, and he must be able to go deep "into the hole" to his right, stop on a dime, and throw hard to first.

That throw from the hole means he must have a strong, accurate arm. Because of that, he usually is the one to handle most relays from left and center fields.

And he must be smart, always thinking one play ahead. Very often the shortstop is the team captain, reminding the others of the possibilities when the ball is hit. More than anyone else, he must anticipate where the ball is likely to go when hit.

How deep should I play? The game situation will dictate this. Most of the time, you'll play deeper than the other infielders, especially against a strong righthanded hitter. But with fewer than two outs and a runner on first, you may move in a little to look for a double play. With a runner on second and a bunt likely, you'll take a step or two toward third so you can get there and cover if the third baseman has to go in to field the bunt.

If the ball is between me and the third baseman, who takes it? The third baseman plays shallower and will usually be in a better position to throw, so he'll take it if he can.

Are there exceptions? There are exceptions to everything. For instance, it's better for you to field a ball standing up than for him to field it stretched out on the ground after diving for it. If you can see this is going to happen, yell that you've got it.

Should I take a pop fly down the third base line? You often have a better angle. You can call off the third baseman when you know you are in a better position. It will be easier for you to cut diagonally and catch a popup than for a third baseman to race down the line with his back to the infield.

How do I know which base to cover? Think.

If the ball is hit to right field and the second baseman goes out for it, you cover second. If he doesn't

make the catch, he'll handle the relay. On a slow hit that he comes in for, or on the occasions when the second baseman covers first, you get to second. Even if there are no runners on base, there may be an overthrow at first.

If the third baseman is away from the bag chasing a ball down the line or one bunted down the baseline with a runner on second, you cover third.

When a ball is hit deep to left or center, don't cover a base, go into the outfield to take a relay.

Runners on base. A ball is hit to me. Where do I throw it? The first rule is get *somebody* out. After that it depends on the situation. With two outs always take the surest out. For example, if you field the ball near second and the runner is coming down from first on a force play, the surest thing for you to do is step on second yourself. If you have to throw, first base is usually the surest. Once in a

Like all other infielders, the shortstop must keep low and stay in front of the ball.

Once he has it, a strong, accurate throw to first base is must.

while, because the throw is shorter, a forceout at second may be easier.

With one or no outs, you should look for a double play.

How should I throw the ball to the second baseman for a double play? It depends on where you get the ball. If you're close to the bag a chest-high underhand toss to the second baseman is best. Don't hide the ball with your glove before throwing. You want the second baseman to see it as early as he can.

If you're farther away, make an overhand throw, again chest-high. Ideally, the second baseman will get the ball just before he reaches the bag.

What do I do if I'm the middleman? Go as hard as you can to second base. Then put on the brakes when you're about two steps from the bag. Try to put yourself, the base, and the second baseman in a line so the second baseman can see you better. Give him a good target with both hands chest-high. After you catch the ball, drag your right foot across the bag and throw to first.

With runners on first and second and one or no outs, the ball is hit to me. Where should I throw for a double play? Are you certain a double play can be made? You may have moved so far to your right that a chance for a double play is lost. Usually on a ball hit to your right, the third baseman has come off to his left and won't be able to get back to cover the bag. Can you tag the baserunner heading for third or outrun him to the bag for a forceout? A double play is great, but be absolutely certain that you get at least one out. And if you have a choice, get the lead runner.

However, if you commit to third, you're virtually giving up any chance to get two. A 6-5-3 double play is unusual. Unless the runner on second is exceptionally slow (or asleep), you'll be able to get the ball to second and on to first quicker than to third and then all the way across the diamond to first. Most of the time on this play, you'll throw to second.

But if you've had to charge way in on a slow hit or if the runners were moving with the pitch, your only sure out may be at first base. Take it.

Naturally, when the ball is hit, you don't have time to consider all these possibilities, so you should have gone over all your options in your mind before the pitch.

What do I do if there's only a runner on second and fewer than two outs? That's different. The runner's not forced to go to third and shouldn't try until he sees what you're going to do with the ball. If he takes off when the ball is hit, you should be able to throw him out on a tag at third unless you have to go so far that you're lucky just to keep the ball in the infield.

On most groundballs, you have time to "look" him back to second, that is, you make a slight hesitation and look at the runner. This should make him stop and begin moving back to the base. If he tries to run after you throw to first, he should be an easy out.

Once in a great while, he'll be so far off second that you can catch him in a pickoff by throwing to the second baseman covering as soon as the runner starts back to the base. Be sure you have him before trying this because if he gets back safely, you'll have two runners on without getting an out.

Is it the same with a runner on third and one or no outs? Basically, yes. But remember that a runner on third is far more likely to run as soon as the ball is hit. Come up ready to throw home or look him back to third, whichever his actions dictate. You want to keep him from scoring if at all possible. If he's gotten such a jump that you can't get him at home, don't throw there just for form, throw the other runner out at first. It's better to allow one run (unless it's the tie-breaker in the last half of the final inning, of course) than to let a "big inning" get started.

What do I do on a pickoff play to second base? The shortstop is usually the one who covers second when the pitcher tries to pick a runner off that base. This is because when the runner watches the pitcher he can still see the second baseman out of the corner of his eye, but to watch the shortstop he must turn his head and take his eye off the pitcher.

The shortstop can sometimes be clear to the bag before the runner knows he's there. If you study the runner, you may be able to pick up a "rhythm" in his looks toward the shortstop that will allow you to dash to second just after he's looked at you.

Straddle the bag facing the runner. Take the throw with both hands if you can. Even if you must catch it with one hand, get your other hand on the ball quickly to protect it. That runner is coming back hard. Make your tag by putting your glove down on the ground between the runner and the base. The back of your hands should be toward the baserunner.

What should I do on a double steal with a runner on third and less than two outs? You don't want that runner to score from third. Let the second baseman cover the bag. You cut toward the center of the diamond while squaring yourself to throw home. You can see the runner out of the corner of your eye while watching the ball. If he goes back to third, let the ball go through to the second baseman. If the runner on third makes any move toward home or is far enough down the line that you think he might go home, you can cut off the catcher's throw.

Now you have to make another decision. If the runner continues for home, throw to the catcher. If the runner turns back toward third, you can throw to the third baseman, who should be on the bag by now. Often the runner will stop, hoping you'll throw one way so he can run the other. In this case run straight at him, forcing him to decide. When he breaks, throw ahead of him for the putout.

What should I do if I catch a runner in a rundown? There are two things that all infielders should be aware of. First always force the runner back toward the base he came from. Second make the putout as quickly as possible with as few throws as possible. Every throw increases the chance of a misplay and every second gives other runners a chance to advance.

Depending on how the play starts, the shortstop may be the key man between the runner and the next base. Let's say you have a man caught off second. The second baseman will cover second and the third baseman will guard third. When you have the ball, you force the runner back toward second. When he breaks for second base (or is too close to it to run to third), you make a soft overhand throw to the second baseman. It should come to him shoulder-high. Incidentally, you shouldn't have to throw over the runner; a simple step to your right should give you a better angle.

If the runner dashes for third, the second baseman will throw back to you. If you've let the runner get so close to you that he may be past you before you get the ball, the second baseman should throw to the third baseman. In that case, you circle around to back up the third baseman while he chases the runner back toward second.

Naturally any time you're close enough to the runner to tag him with the ball, do so. But don't find yourself chasing him back to the base when you can't catch him.

Shortstop tips

Ozzie Smith was the N.L.'s Gold Glove choice at shortstop every year in the 1980s—ten straight! His acrobatic play set the standard by which every shortstop will be judged from now on.

Ozzie says: "Field grounders near the instep of your left foot if you can; that's my style. Always be sure to get squarely in front of hard-hit groundballs. The ball won't bite you—and you're wearing a glove so it won't hurt when you stop it."

In the last two seasons Pittsburgh's Jay Bell has solidified the shortstop position, which was once considered a Pirate weakness. His steady play has improved the Buccos' defense. Jay says, "The pitch will affect where the ball goes, so I always watch the sign. That enables me to 'cheat' one way or the other on which way I'll break.

"Charge the ball. Be aggressive. If you lay

back, you don't play the ball, the ball plays you.

"Stay low and keep your hands low and away from your body. It's easier to come up—even leap—than to suddenly jab down for a ball that takes a surprise low bounce.

If you have lots of time, you can even go down to one knee to field the ball."

In starting a double play, Bell says: "I do everything the same in fielding the ball—with one exception. I field the ball to the righthand side of my body so I can get the throw away quicker. Speed is important in making a double play."

Terry Pendleton is a two-time Gold Glove winner at third base for the St. Louis Cardinals.

CHAPTER 10

Playing Third Base

What abilities do I need to be a third baseman?
You need a strong, accurate arm because you make so many long throws across the diamond, although the shortstop sometimes makes even longer throws. Moreover, you must be able to get the ball away quickly.

Foot speed is not important. Several outstanding third basemen have been slow runners. But you must be able to react like a shot. The ball often gets down to third base so quickly that any hesitation on your part will allow it to go through. In fact, there's often only enough time to knock the ball down with your glove, scramble after it, and fire to first.

Be alert!

Is that why they call it the "hot corner"? Yes, things happen fast at third base. You have to be ready. And many games turn on the third baseman's ability to move and think quickly.

Where should I line up? The third baseman usually lines up only a step or two deeper than the base and about ten feet inside the baseline, but if you are expecting a bunt, you may move in several steps. On righthanded pull-hitters, you should move closer to the baseline because any well-hit ball that goes past between you and the base will almost certainly go for a double. Many managers move their third baseman even closer to the line in late innings, when an extra-base hit could mean the ball game.

Balls hit down the third base line are some of the hardest plays for a third baseman to make because they are often hit hard and require a very long throw.

When a ball is hit between short and third, who handles it? The third baseman is closer to the batter and should handle anything he can get his hands on.

What do I do on a slow roller or a bunt? These are often "do or die" plays. Many third basemen feel these are the hardest plays for a third baseman to make. You charge in fast, actually run past the ball on the left, reach down with your right hand, pick it up, and throw in the same motion. This is a very tricky play, and you should practice it over and over before you try to do it in a game.

Isn't it better sometimes to let the ball roll? Yes. Bunts particularly have a tendency to roll foul when they start near the foul line. Stay close to the ball, and the second it rolls into foul territory brush it farther foul with your glove.

Do I come in on every bunt? No. If there's a runner on second and the ball is bunted where the pitcher can get it, you should get back to third base fast for a possible play on the runner.

How do I make a forceout at third? Whenever possible, step across the bag toward first and drag your right foot over the bag. This puts you in position to throw to first base. Much of the time you won't have much chance to do anything more than get to the bag and tag it with whatever foot gets there first.

Where do I stand to make a tag on a runner at third? Stand just behind the base so you can easily put the ball down between the runner and the base.

The third baseman should be standing just behind third base when putting the tag on a runner.

Hot tips from the hot corner

Terry Pendleton has won two Gold Gloves as the St. Louis Cardinals third baseman. He's known for his strong arm and his quickness. He stresses practice. "I was moved to third base in 1984. It took a heck of a lot of hard work to learn the position. It helps to have talent, but there's no substitute for hard work. I've made some plays at third base [that] I can't explain how I made them. All I can say is that from practice, I had the necessary reactions."

Terry adds, "I take a step in as the ball is pitched. Some players stand there without moving, but I like to get a rhythm going. I'm on balance. I'm comfortable. You can't push me over, but I can go any way I want to, left, right, or back.

"My biggest asset," Terry says, "is I try to be as accurate as possible and as quick as possible. I try to allow myself time to make an error. Then, if I drop the ball, I have time to pick it up; if I make a bad throw, the first baseman has time to go get it and get back to the bag."

On relays from the outfield "I run out waving my arms," Pendleton says, "so the outfielder has no trouble seeing me. As the ball comes in, I catch it on my glove side. This is important because I can get my throw away faster."

Pittsburgh Pirate catcher Mike LaValliere won a Gold Glove in 1988 for his stellar defensive work behind the plate.

Catching

They used to call the catcher's equipment the "tools of ignorance," suggesting that anyone who'd go behind the plate and let people throw baseballs at him must be a little short on smarts. Just the opposite is true, of course. A catcher, more than any other fielder, must keep his head in the game. No doubt that's why so many catchers have gone on to successful postplaying careers as managers and coaches.

I'm a slow runner. Should I become a catcher? A catcher doesn't need to be a particularly fast runner. But the position demands several other abilities. In fact, many people believe it is the toughest position of all.

Do you know baseball? The catcher has to be smart about the game. He's the only defensive player who can see the whole field at one time. He not only calls the pitches, he is also the quarterback on many plays telling the other players what to do.

Are you durable? The catcher wears more and heavier equipment than any other player. He must squat to give his signs, then crouch before every pitch. Can you do that a hundred times? He'll catch most of the pitches, and even when a pitch doesn't get to him because a batter hits it, he'll start to catch it. He goes after popup fouls and tags runners at the plate. A catcher is the hardest-working player on the field.

Do you have a strong arm? Every time you catch a pitch, you must throw the ball back to the pitcher—if you're not throwing to a base. That's sixty feet to the pitcher, ninety feet to the first or third baseman, and 120 feet when you throw to second base. Naturally, accuracy is a must.

And, even though you don't have to run very fast, you need "quick" feet because you so often have to move fast to block bad pitches.

Does a catcher have to wear all that heavy equipment? In a game you'd be crazy not to wear all your equipment. Every piece of a catcher's equipment is designed to protect you from serious injury. No matter how well you catch, you can't know ahead of time where a foul tip will go.

Starting at the top, you should wear a helmet. It

Communicating which pitch you want the pitcher to throw is done by showing any number of fingers.

Before the pitch comes in, provide a good target for the pitcher showing exactly where you want the ball.

looks like a batting helmet without earflaps. Some are made with no bill. An obvious example of why you need one: the pitch is low; you reach down, dropping your head, and the batter foul tips into your head above your mask. With a helmet, you hardly feel it; without a helmet, they carry you away.

The Little League model mask attaches directly to the helmet to provide continuous protection.

Do you know what they call someone who catches without a mask? Gums! Of course, if you'd like to be toothless and have your nose smashed, you might go behind the plate without a mask. Except that no coach would play a catcher that dumb. If your mask isn't equipped with an extension to protect your throat, get one.

A sturdy chest protector will save you a lot of bruises and even cracked ribs. Make certain it fits snugly. If it droops, a foul tip can find a gap. In Little League, a long-model chest protector with a neck collar (to protect the throat area) is mandatory.

An athletic supporter with a metal, plastic, or fiber cup protector is an absolute must for boys. Because this is worn under the uniform, it might not be noticed by your coach if you forget. So for heaven's sake don't forget! Most coaches make a point of checking that you're protected, but don't rely on

other people; *you* remember!

Shin guards obviously protect you from painful shots to the shins, but they also guard your knees and ankles.

The reason for the extra padding a catcher's mitt has is apparent to anyone who ever caught a fastball.

How do I give signs to the pitcher? Before every pitch you squat down to give the pitcher the sign. Keep your feet close together and your legs spread. Your glove is held on your left knee so the third base coach can't see the sign. Your right hand is against the inside of your right thigh to hide the sign from the first base coach. Be careful not to let your hand drop too low or someone behind you can see your fingers.

Can I stay in my squat to catch the pitch? No, in a squat you're in no position to throw, to come out fast for a ball hit or bunted in front of the plate, or to chase back for a pop foul.

How should I stand to receive pitches? Get in a deep crouch with your feet spread apart a comfortable distance. One of the big things in your catching position is balance. Your weight is on the balls of your feet, not back on your haunches. Some catchers keep their left foot in front for better balance and to help them get ready to throw. Get close to the plate but out of the batter's way. Your tail shouldn't be too high or too low.

Give the pitcher a good target.

Hold your mitt up, steady and open to give the pitcher a good target. Show him exactly where you want the pitch. Keep your elbows out.

Always protect your bare hand. Your bare hand is held beside the mitt, ready to close over the ball. Keep your hand relaxed in a loose fist. If you open your hand and extend your fingers when a pitch is on the way, they could be injured by a foul tip.

How can I improve my throwing? Accuracy is most important. You have to work on quickness and accuracy until you find what works for you. Thurman Munson (former New York Yankees catcher) threw to second base from about 15 different arm angles. A lot depends on the person. Benito Santiago (of the San Diego Padres) has a tremendous arm. He's thrown out runners from a kneeling position. He doesn't have to be quick. Others, such Pittsburgh's Mike LaValliere, whose arms aren't as strong, must rely on quickness.

There's no one set way to do it, but you should start with fundamentals until you develop your own style.

You should be able to catch the ball and shift into throwing position in one smooth motion. Your footwork gets you ready. As you catch the ball, your weight shifts to your right foot. Don't straighten up before you throw. A catcher can't afford to wind up before throwing: bring the ball up to ear level, step forward with your left foot, and fire. Make your throws overhand; sidearm throws tend to curve.

Accuracy is more important than the speed with which the ball gets there. Accuracy comes by practicing a lot. Develop accuracy by always throwing to a player at second base.

Should I wait until I see a fielder on the base before I throw it? If you're making a surprise throw to a base with no sign given, you'll surprise your fielder as much as the runner, so, of course, you must throw only when the fielder is close to the bag. That still gives you plenty of opportunity to chase runners back to their bases with throws.

But if the sign for a pickoff throw is given or if a runner is trying to steal, you don't have time to wait for an infielder to get to the base. For example, when throwing to second, aim for a spot knee-high above the center of the bag. The infielder will get there before the ball arrives.

Do I need to know anything about return throws to the pitcher? Practice throwing back to the pitcher. Overthrows and underthrows can allow a runner to take an extra base."

Throws to bases are dramatic, but your pitch-after-pitch return throws to the pitcher are important, too. If you're constantly making your pitcher jump for or reach for your throws, you'll tire him out.

How do I catch a popup? Find the ball. And don't run around looking all over for it. Find it first; then move.

You're too close to follow its flight off the bat, but here's a tip: righthanded hitters foul outside pitches to your right, inside pitches to your left. Lefthanded hitters will foul outside pitches to your left, inside to your right. If you are aware of this, you'll know where to look for the ball.

Get your mask off immediately, but don't throw it away yet. You may have to run in the direction you threw your mask while looking up—a good way to create a disaster. Once you spot the ball, throw your mask away and well behind you.

If an infielder can handle a pop fly, let him. Listen for his call. Most of the popups you'll be responsible for will be behind the plate.

You should know that popups behind the plate tend to drift back toward the infield, but it's easier to come in on a ball than to back up, so stay back and come to it.

Should I catch pop flies with my mitt over my head? No. Always hold your glove face up when settling under pop flies. Infielders and outfielders catch flies with their hands up, but a catcher wears a different kind of mitt. Catch the ball out in front with your palms up. That way you can "look" the ball into your mitt, and, if necessary, smother it against your chest protector.

After you catch a popup with men on base, run the ball back to the infield. Don't forget, a runner can tag up and run on any pop fly.

What do I do on a ball hit or bunted right in front of the plate? Come out from behind the plate fast, flipping your mask up over your forehead so it falls behind you. On a play like that, you can see the whole play in front of you—where the runners are in relation to the bases, where the fielders are. Before the play starts, know the number of runners and outs, so you already know what to look for. Depending on what your fielders do, make the decision on who's going to make the play and where he should throw the ball. Then yell. When you take

On a popup, catch the ball in front of you with your palm up and look the ball into your mitt.

the play yourself, reach down with two hands, stopping the ball with your mitt and grasping it with your bare hand. You crow-hop toward the base you're going to throw to and let it fly.

What are some of the other "quarterbacking" things a catcher does? Before you give the sign, remind your fielders of the number of outs, the runners on base, whether a bunt or steal is likely, and to look for a double play when a runner is on first.

Warn the pitcher if his mechanics start to slip. For example, if he's not following through.

When a ball is hit, you call for a particular infielder to take a pop fly or tell the fielder where to throw. If an infielder is chasing a foul pop, tell him how much room he has. If a ball is hit to the right with no runner in scoring position, you run down the first base line to back up the first baseman on an over-throw.

On a throw coming in from the outfield to the plate, you yell to the cutoff man if he should take the throw or let it go through.

Why do I call the pitch? I'm not the one who'll throw it. First, you want to know what's coming so you can catch it. Second, you have a better view of the pitch than he does, so you know what's working. And third, two heads are better than one—especially if your head has been busy studying the batters.

What kinds of signs do you give the pitcher? Typically one finger for a fastball, two for a curve, and so on. Of course at your level, the pitcher shouldn't risk his arm by throwing curves, but he may throw an off-speed pitch. Before the game, talk over what the signs will be with your pitcher. And if a new pitcher comes into the game, go out to the mound to talk it over with him.

What if the pitcher can only throw fastballs? The other team doesn't know that. Give a sign anyway and keep them guessing. And, of course, you may want to call for a pitchout.

What's a pitchout? That's when the pitcher intentionally throws the ball wide of the plate to make sure the batter can't hit it. You call it with a special sign worked out in advance. As the pitch is delivered, you step out and away from the plate.

Can't a runner on second base see the signs? Yes. You may want to change them. An easy way might be to give several signs with only the second one counting on the second batter, the third sign counting for the third batter, and so on.

Must the pitcher always throw what I tell him? He can shake off a sign. You want your pitcher to have confidence in what he's going to throw. If you're convinced you have the right call, give him the same sign again. If he still shakes you off, go to another pitch.

Do you have any tips on choosing pitches? Bob Boone, who's caught more games than any other catcher in major league history, has one: "When you play a team, jot down (after the game) a note to yourself concerning the team's best hitters. Did the batter swing at high pitches? Did another batter try to hit low pitches? The next time your pitcher faces that batter, you may be able to call for a pitch that will get a big out."

How do I catch bad pitches? You always want to move in front of a pitch rather than reach out or catch it backhand. You should practice your footwork.

On a pitch to your left, step left with your left foot and drop your right foot back to be ready to throw. On a pitch to your right, you step out and back with your right foot and then move your left foot. In other

When a pitch is thrown in the dirt to one side, the catcher must shift over to block the pitch. The most important thing to remember is to always stay in front of the ball.

words, do not cross one leg over the other; step off with the foot toward the pitch and then bring the other foot into position to make a throw.

Here's a tip: if the pitch is just out of the strike zone, don't shift. Catch it and pull it in; the umpire may call it a strike.

How should I handle balls that bounce in front of the plate? Blocking low balls can be difficult. You've got to keep your glove down, put your knees on the ground, and block the ball. Keep that ball in front of you in whatever way you can, with your glove, your knees, or your chest. Tuck in your chin. Even with a mask, a bouncing ball can hop up and hit you in the throat. You can't be scared of the ball. If you always have the ball in full view, you and your team are not going to get hurt by low pitches.

Ray Fosse, a former All Star catcher, has suggested a good drill for blocking balls in the dirt: "Have someone stand about ten feet in front of you and throw the ball in the dirt to your right and left.

In one drill, field about fifteen balls on each side, then fifteen straight at you, still in the dirt."

How do I block the plate to make tag plays? On a throw coming from left field, wait in fair territory near the first base line. On a throw from right field, wait in foul territory, a step toward third base. Naturally if a throw is bad, you move out and get it.

When you catch the ball, drop to one or both knees between the runner and the plate. Hold the ball in two hands with the back of your glove toward the runner. Keep the ball low so the runner must slide into it.

How do I make a force play? This only happens when the bases are loaded and usually with one or no outs, so you're looking for a double play. Put your right foot on the plate. As soon as you catch the ball, step toward first base. Make your throw to the inside of first base so the runner won't interfere with the first baseman's ability to catch the ball.

Backstop tips

Pittsburgh Pirate catcher Mike LaValliere won a Gold Glove in 1988 for his stellar play behind the plate. The stocky receiver (called "Spanky" for his resemblance to Spanky McFarlane of the "Our Gang Comedies" films) is known for his easy-going sense of humor, but he takes playing his position very seriously.

"I'd recommend wearing at least your mask even when you're only warming up a pitcher," LaValliere says.

"When you're first starting out it's a good idea to have all your equipment on whenever you can so you can get used to it. Your equipment should become like a second skin. Naturally, you must find equipment that fits you properly—your glove, mask, chest protector, shin guards, and so on—so you can feel comfortable."

Mike explains how he built up his legs for all the squatting and crouching a catcher must do:

"When I was younger and I wanted to go some place, I had a stubborn mother who knew what was best for me. So I didn't get driven in a car—I walked or rode my bicycle. That's how I got back and forth to my Little League games. Also I grew up in New Hampshire where we played hockey. Skating was awfully good for my legs."

He's known as one of the best at working with his pitchers on pitch selection. "I call every pitch—I don't get any directions from the dugout. I call pitch by pitch; each pitch dictates the next. We have a general game plan and it's my job to vary from it as the need arises."

He says kids always ask him how to keep from blinking when they catch the ball. "Don't worry about it," he tells them. "I didn't believe I blinked until I saw it on a feature on national TV. I guess the majority of catchers blink on some pitches. So if a youngster blinks, he shouldn't be ashamed of it. We do it in the major leagues."

CHAPTER 12

Playing the Outfield

A famous major league manager once said that outfielders should have to pay to get into the ballpark. His point was that outfielders make fewer plays than the pitcher or other fielders and the great majority of those plays outfielders do make during the course of a game are pretty routine.

True enough.

It's not unusual for an outfielder to go through a whole game and never handle the ball. He may go several games without doing more than catching a few easy flyballs and running down singles hit through the infield.

But when an infielder makes a mistake, opponents usually get a base; when an outfielder makes a mistake, it often means a run for the other side. The outfielder is the last line of defense. He's expected to make all the ordinary plays without fail. But the great outfielders can do more than that. When you watch the highlight films on TV news, think how often they show remarkable game-saving catches by outfielders.

What do I do out there? First, stay alert. It's so easy to relax out in the outfield where you're so far away from much of the game's action. You might stand there for several innings without getting a single play. Under those circumstances you'll be tempted to straighten up, to put your hands on your hips, and to start thinking about what you'll do after the game.

What is the most important play for an outfielder? Surprisingly it's fielding grounders. Not very exciting. It's pretty routine on most plays. Sometimes the television cameras don't even bother to follow the ball into the outfield on ordinary singles, preferring to focus on the runner racing to first base.

But if the outfielder doesn't make his routine play—field the grounder and throw it in—it can turn into a most exciting play, with the embarrassed outfielder galloping back to the fence after the ball he let get by him and the runner happily zipping around the bases.

During most games an outfielder will handle more grounders than flyballs, yet few young outfielders

One of the most important plays for an outfielder is the groundball; a muff means extra bases.

It takes lots of practice to learn to judge where a flyball is going.

spend much time practicing their most important type of play.

The ball is bouncing toward me. What now? The basics of fielding grounders are mostly the same for infielders and outfielders: get in front of the ball, charge it if you can, try to take it on a good bounce, and use two hands. Whenever you can, go down on one knee to field a grounder. That will keep it from bouncing between your knees. Usually you have plenty of time to do this and still make your throw.

The ball is in the air? What do I do? It's more a question of what did you do before? There's no way to learn to judge and catch flies except to judge and catch flies. Have a coach or friend hit you fly after fly after fly. During batting practice, go to your regular outfield position and practice fielding. The balls hit in batting practice will come at you like

those in a real game, but you don't have to worry if you misjudge one. Gradually, through practice, you'll gain confidence.

How do I get a good "jump" on the ball? Expect every pitch to be hit toward you. Lean forward on the balls of your feet, your glove ready, your head in the game. Think about the number of outs and where any runners are likely to go if the ball comes your way. What will you do?

You watch the pitch. Some outfielders say they watch the batter. Willie Wilson of the Kansas City Royals says, "What I do is just watch the bat—just the bat." With practice, when the ball comes off the bat, you'll know where it's going to come down. Run to that spot, and—sure enough—here it comes.

Always catch the ball with two hands when possible. Some major leaguers make stylish, one-handed catches on routine flies, but don't forget, they caught thousands of flyballs safely before they ever tried to get fancy.

What about throwing the ball? Let's start with how the ball should come back to the infield. On most throws, the important thing is to get the ball in fast.

Most of an outfielder's throws are long. Young players tend to throw the ball high, in a big "rainbow" arc so it will go farther. Unfortunately, while the infielders are waiting for the throw to come down, the runners are racing merrily around the bases. A ball thrown on a line, even if it bounces a couple of times, will get to the infield faster than a rainbow. Equally important, an infielder can cutoff a low throw and whip it to a base to catch an unwary runner.

This is something that can't be stressed enough: keep your throws on a low line!

Is there a trick to throwing well from the outfield? It's not exactly a trick. It's simply something you should do on every play that you can. When you catch a fly or field a grounder, you should already be moving toward the infield. On grounders charge the ball. On lazy flies move to a position a step or so behind where you want to make the catch and then move in at the last second. This way, your momentum is already going toward the infield.

Once you've secured the ball, take a little hop step (sometimes called a "crow-hop") so you can really get your weight moving forward as you throw.

Some outfielders will catch the ball off their throwing shoulder so they won't waste time bringing the ball across their body before throwing.

Which base do I throw to? This can get very complicated. It depends on the number of runners, their speed, and the game situation. There are a few simple rules. Never throw to a base the runner already occupies or is just about to occupy. Most of the time you won't throw to a base, you'll throw to an infielder who will come out to take the ball: the left fielder throws to the shortstop, the right fielder throws to the second baseman, and the center fielder throws to the infielder nearest second base.

Don't I ever throw home? Very seldom. This is where you'll often see even very smart outfielders make a mistake: There's a runner on second and the ball is hit to medium depth in one of the alleys. The outfielder cuts off the hit and thinks, "Wouldn't it be great to throw that runner out at the plate?" He forgets all his practice and makes that big old rainbow throw—and the runner scores easily. What he should have done, of course, was make a strong, low throw to the infielder (who will have lined himself up with the plate). If the throw is terrific, the infielder can let it go right on through to home. Otherwise he can cut it off and either relay it on (which often gets the ball there faster) or let the run go and stop any other runner from advancing.

About the only time an outfielder throws straight for the plate, without worrying about a cut-off man, is when the runner is on second and the outfielder fields a ball hit in front of him or when the only runner is on third and the outfielder comes in for a fly. And even in that situation, only throw to the plate if the runner has tagged and is racing home. There is no use risking an overthrow if the runner isn't going to try to score.

Can I relax on groundballs to the infield? Certainly not! Even the "easiest" grounders bounce through sometime. You must move to back up the infielder in front of you as soon as the ball is hit. Nine times out of ten, you won't be needed, but the tenth time you may save the game.

What about balls hit to the other outfielders? Always back up the outfielder near you. If you're already moving on a ball that bounces past him, you'll be able to get there faster than he will. A quick backup can mean the difference between the runner getting two bases and four.

Are the same abilities needed for all three outfield positions? All outfielders have to run and throw, so the faster the feet and the stronger the arm the better. Still, if you had three players to choose from for the three outfield positions, you'd probably do it this way (assuming they could all catch the ball):

Put your fastest man in center field because he has the most occasion to make long runs. His speed can also help him cover some of the territory in the power alleys for a particularly slow outfielder on either side.

Put your strongest arm in right field because he will have to make the longest throws. He'll also get more action than the left fielder if your pitcher has good speed; there will be more righthanded batters swinging late.

Left field requires fewer long throws and may not be quite as busy as center or right, but that doesn't mean it's not an important defensive position. If the left fielder is weak, you can bet that your opponent will soon discover that and purposely try to hit the ball to him.

A "Wynne-ing" tip

In his eight major league seasons, Marvell Wynne of the Cubs has played all three outfield positions.

"People ask me what's the biggest difference between playing the infield and playing the outfield," Wynne says. "I tell them you can relax more in the outfield. But you still must be alert. You've got to pay attention to the game situation, keep an eye on the batter, think ahead to where you'll throw the ball if it's hit to you—it's like going to school out there—be ready!"

Marvell Wynne of the Chicago Cubs.

PART 3

Strategy
and Training

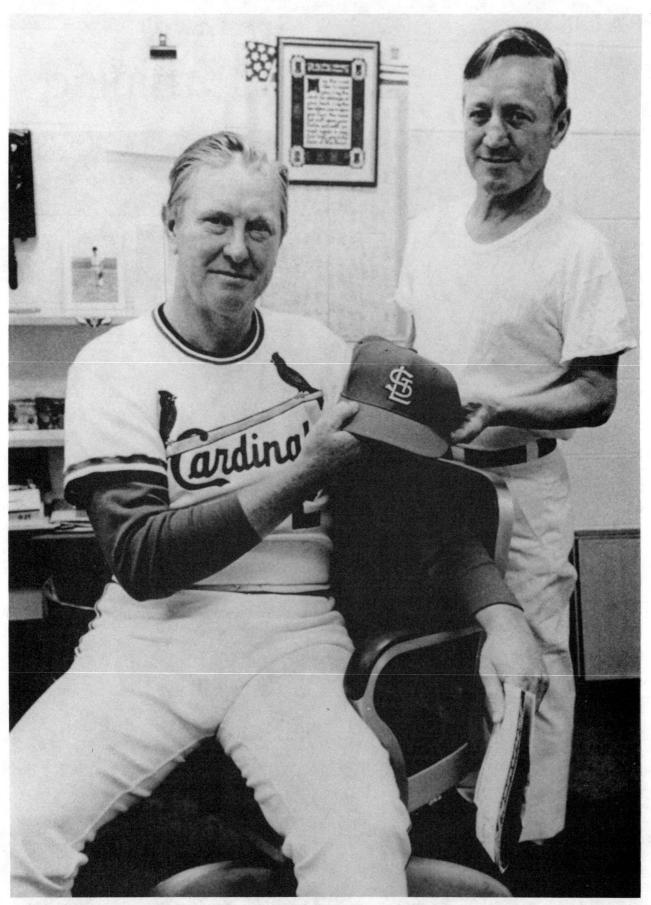

Red Schoendienst managed the St. Louis Cardinals for thirteen years and is still an active coach for the team. As manager, he has had to make thousands of strategy decisions.

CHAPTER 13

Strategy

As a young player you won't make strategy decisions for your team. That's the manager's job. Still, it's important that you know what kinds of strategic decisions he may make and why—and, in some cases, what you must do in response to decisions made by the other team's manager.

Red Schoendienst was an outstanding National League second baseman from 1945 to 1963 with the Cardinals, Braves, and Giants. As manager of the Cardinals, for thirteen years, he led his team to two pennants and a world championship in 1967. Still an active Cardinals coach after nearly fifty years of major league baseball, Red was named to the Hall of Fame in 1989.

What kinds of decisions do managers make?
Before the game the manager makes out the lineup. During the game he decides on pinch hitters and substitutes. One of his most important jobs is determining when to change pitchers. He's also responsible for game strategy, when to bunt or hit-and-run, for example. Minor league and youth league managers must also be able to teach youngsters how to play their positions. And, above all, managers at all levels must keep their players alert and ready.

What should a manager look for in making out his lineup? The first or lead-off hitter should be good at getting on base. He'll usually have more at bats than any other batter, so he shouldn't waste them. He need not hit a lot of home runs or even have a very high batting average if he can draw a lot of walks. His job is to be on base so that someone else can drive him in. It's a real bonus if the lead-off man is a good base stealer like the Cardinals' Vince Coleman because once he's on first, there's a good chance he'll steal second where he can score on a single.

The second hitter should be a good handler of the bat. He's often called on to sacrifice or hit behind the runner. He should avoid strikeouts and hopefully hit the ball on the ground more often than in the air.

The third batter is likely to be the best all-around hitter on the team. He may not have the most power, but he should have some. Most of all, he should be able to drive that man in from second base.

The fourth hitter is called the clean-up man because that's what you hope he can do—clean the bases. This is the man you want to hit the home run because, with three good hitters in front of him, that homer should be good for more than a single run.

The fifth and sixth hitters are often power hitters, too. As you descend through the batting order, batters will have fewer and fewer at bats, so if you had three hitters with equal power, you'd arrange them fourth through sixth according to their likelihood of getting on base, with the fourth man the most likely.

The last three spots in the order are usually for the team's weakest hitters. But that doesn't mean those spots are not important. Good teams almost always have some punch at the bottom.

How should a manager choose a pinch hitter? Curveballs dictate a lot of this strategy at higher levels. Of course, at your level, pitchers shouldn't be throwing curves, so the manager is likely to simply send up the best available batter for a given situation—for example, a good "on-base" man to lead off an inning, a good bunter if a sacrifice is called for, or a power hitter if a home run is desperately needed.

But let's talk about how those curves affect choices so you'll understand why the manager of your favorite big league team makes some of his choices.

A righthanded pitcher's curve breaks away from a righthanded batter. That makes it harder for a righthanded batter to hit it than for a lefty. Therefore, a manager will often choose a pinch hitter with a lower batting average just because of the side of the plate he bats from. For example, with a righthander on the mound, he may send up a lefthanded .250 hitter instead of a righthanded .280 hitter. Managers look at batter statistics showing what different batters do against different kinds of pitching. The .250 lefthanded hitter may actually be a .300 hitter against righthanded pitching.

Is the same lefty-righty idea used in bringing in a new pitcher? On the major league level, it's more important. A manager may bring in a lefty reliever to face a lefthanded hitter. However, on your level there are different considerations. For example, a manager wouldn't want to bring in a relief pitcher who's fast but wild if the bases were loaded.

Can you describe a "bunt situation"? "The usual bunt situation," says St. Louis Cardinal coach Red Schoendienst, "happens when your team is one run down, tied, or only a run or two ahead—times when getting a single run is important. Suppose you have a runner on first and no one out. It's worth giving up an out to move that runner up a base, especially if one of your weaker hitters is up at bat.

"The defense knows the situation, of course. So when the batter squares around to bunt, the defense reacts. The first and third basemen charge in for the ball. The second baseman races over to cover first base. The shortstop covers second.

"Bunts also occur with runners on second or on first *and* second. One thing the infielders must remember is whether the lead runner can be put out by a force or if he must be tagged."

What about stealing bases? When Schoendienst was playing, the stolen base wasn't used very often. Although Red led the National League in steals with 26 in 1945, he only swiped 62 more over the next eighteen seasons. But as a manager, he helped make baserunning a big and exciting part of the game by unleashing Lou Brock. During Red's years as Cardinal manager, Brock led the league in stolen bases eight times.

Modern baserunners are likely to run any time they think they can be successful, but the classic steal situation, according to Red, is similar to the bunt situation—a close game and a runner on first. The only difference is that a steal is likely whether there's none, one, or two outs.

"The second baseman and shortstop decide which one will cover second according to the pitch and the batter," Red says. "On a fastball to a righthanded hitter, he's likely to hit it to the first base side, so the shortstop covers second. Even then the fielders have to be careful and watch out for a hit-and-run play."

What's a hit-and-run play? "It's actually more run-and-then-hit. It's used to stay out of a double play. The runner on first takes off for second, the fielder goes over to cover, and the batter grounds the ball right through where he was standing only a moment before. A good bat handler can often get a hit on a ball that should be an out if he can tell which fielder will cover second.

"The only defense is to disguise which fielder will cover until the last moment. I used to tell the shortstop when I'd cover by holding my glove in front of my face and signaling with the old open-mouth-I-got-it, closed-mouth-it's-yours. Then I'd wait as long as I possibly could before racing to cover second."

How much difference can strategy make in a game? Red and every other manager who ever lived would agree that it can help in a close game. But to win consistently, a team needs good players who play hard.

Little leaguers and major leaguers alike need to stretch and warm up before they even pick up a baseball. It may seem routine and boring, but warm-ups are among the most important things you must do.

CHAPTER 14

Training

Injuries are bound to happen if you play baseball. You'll get minor injuries. What you want to prevent are *serious* injuries. And there are three things you can do to help.

First, always wear proper equipment and wear it properly.

Second, practice proper playing techniques.

And third, warm up properly before you start to play.

That last one can fool you. What do you do when you warm up? Throw the ball a couple times to get your arm ready?

Wrong!

Before you even touch a baseball, get your body ready with a few good stretching exercises. That's how big leaguers minimize pulled muscles that can put them on the bench. Come to the ballpark early some time, long before batting practice. You'll see the players out on the field going through their stretching exercises, getting their bodies ready to play ball.

Stretching exercises are not the same thing as calisthenics. We're not talking about building Marines here. No fifty push-ups, please! The purpose is simply to get the muscles loose. It's not competitive; you stretch to the point of discomfort and that's all.

In an article for *Play Ball with Little League,* Gus Hoefling, the Philadelphia Phillies' fitness trainer,

Disclaimer: Consult Your Doctor First

On this and the following pages you'll find suggestions for exercises and treatment of minor injuries. The instructions and advice presented are in no way intended as a substitute for medical treatment or advice. Consult your doctor before attempting any of the exercises or treatments presented here, especially if you have any serious medical condition or are taking medication.

Major League Baseball®, the author, editors, and publisher of this book must disclaim all responsibility for any injury or illness that may result from employing any treatment or exercise described in this book.

Neck Roll

Shoulder Rotation

ticked off nine good stretching exercises.

Don't be discouraged if you have trouble doing them at first. Lots of people can't touch their toes, for example, until they've built up to it. Do the exercises smoothly; never jerk or lurch.

1. **Neck Rolls:** Stand straight with your legs spread slightly. Loosen up. Drop your head toward your chest and rotate your neck to the right. Continue rolling your head in a circular motion ten times. Then roll it to the left 10 times.

2. **Shoulder Rotations:** Stand with your feet spread about 6 inches wider than your shoulders. Roll your shoulders downward while bringing your arms up in front of you with the backs of your hands facing each other. Then roll your shoulders up and back while bringing your arms behind you with the palms facing each other. Continue to do it 15 times.

3. **Waist Twist:** Plant your feet firmly with your knees slightly bent. Twist to the right, bringing your left arm around with your palm facing up. Repeat to the left with your right arm around, palm up. Make it a continuous motion. Repeat 20 times.

4. **Toe Touches:** Stand pigeon-toed. Extend your arms over your head. Bend forward and try to touch your toes while keeping your legs straight. Repeat 15 times.

5. **Toe Grabs:** Stand with your feet well apart. Turn your body and your feet to the right. Keep your weight on your left leg (slightly bent) while bending to grab your right toes with both hands. Keep your right leg straight. Hold for 5 seconds. Repeat 10 times for each leg.

6. **Lower Groin Stretch:** Stand with your legs spread, knees slightly bent. Keep your hands in front. Transfer your weight to your left leg as you squat. Straighten up and switch to your right leg. Repeat 10 times.

Waist Twist

Toe Touches

Toe Grabs

Lower Groin Stretch

Hurdle Stretch

Elbow to Knees

Sit-Ups

7. **Hurdle Stretch:** Sit in a hurdle position with your left leg straight out in front, heel pushed forward, and your right leg bent so that your foot is behind you. Touch your left toe with your right hand. Twist and touch your right heel with your left hand. Repeat 15 times, then switch legs.

8. **Elbow to Knees:** Sit down and spread your legs wide. Lock your hands behind your head. Keep your legs as straight as you can and touch your right knee with your left elbow. Then your left knee with your right elbow. Alternate left and right 20 times.

9. **Sit-Ups:** Lie on your back with your feet together and your arms back over your head. Sit up and try to touch your toes. Hold it for 3 seconds. Lie down. Repeat 20 times.

At first some of these may seem a little hard. Remember, don't push it. When it starts to hurt a little, that's enough. After a few sessions it'll get easier. Eventually you'll be able to do all of these exercises without even thinking about them.

And don't forget, these would be worth doing even if you skipped playing baseball.

No matter how well you train, you're going to get an occasional little ache, pain, or strain. What do you do about it? Remember, we're not talking about a serious hurt here—for those, see a person qualified to treat you. We just want to deal with those annoying little ouches.

Major leaguers use *RICE*.

No, not the stuff that grows in paddies and gets thrown at weddings. *RICE* stands for Rest, Ice, Compression, and Elevation.

To put it simply:

First immobilize the injured area. If your leg hurts, it *won't* help to run on it. *Rest* it.

Next apply *Ice* to the injured area.

By *Compression*, we mean tie it on so it stays.

And finally *Elevate* the injured area on a chair or table or whatever. Raise it to get the blood flowing.

Treat those little injuries with *RICE* and you'll be ready to play again before you know it.

PHOTO CREDITS

Courtesy of the Chicago Cubs: p. 42 right, 44, 76.

David Liam Kyle: p. 48.

National Baseball Library: p. 1, 2, 4 top, 18.

Courtesy Pittsburgh Pirates: p. 42 left, 66.

Rawlings Sporting Goods: p. 77.

Courtesy San Francisco Giants: p. 28.

TV Sports Mailbag: p. 33, 34, 56, 62.

Cover photos by Tom DiPace, top, Ron Vesely, center, Louis DeLuca, bottom left.

All other photos by Mike Saporito.